THE MAK

"Frustrated with our polarized culture? Take this incredibly fun ride through the life of modern-day Renaissance man Vikram Mansharamani to appreciate a simple solution—open-minded, generalist thinking. This book is an enjoyable read that lays out a viable path to move beyond today's identity-driven, label-dominated world."
—**Christopher T. Sununu**, *Governor*, State of New Hampshire

"*The Making of a Generalist* touched my heart and made me think differently. Vikram fought the pressures of conventional specialization and chose to embrace the breadth of knowledge that comes with being a generalist. Readers will come away appreciating the value of choosing their own path and thinking for themselves. Moreover, the reader will learn that uncertainty is just an opportunity to learn, grow and innovate."
—**Kim Lew**, *President and Chief Executive Officer*, Columbia Investment Management Company

"As always Vikram makes you think differently. What is important is that you take the time to read this and reflect. Pick this up, you will be mesmerized."
—**General Lori Robinson, USAF (Retired)**, *Former Commander*, NORAD

"Mansharamani documents with an insightful look in the mirror the openness and curiosity that provides foundational strength for generalists. He demonstrates the confidence required to consider other perspectives and in doing so encourages all of us to have a broader, more optimistic view of what's possible. A delightful and ultimately encouraging read!"
—**Michael McCarthy**, *Chairman*, Union Pacific Corporation; *Chairman*, The McCarthy Group

"As a modern-day Indiana Jones, Vikram braves the wilds of today's uncertain world with remarkable tenacity and a devout commitment to identifying opportunities within risks. The generalist approach he models can help each of us create a better future for ourselves, our families, and quite possibly, our country."
—**David Tice**, *President*, Paul Revere Films

"*The Making of a Generalist* is a timely reminder that America is a land of unlimited opportunity. Vikram's story, which would have been impossible in any other nation, demonstrates how an open mind and commitment to learning can empower you to blaze your own trail. A truly inspiring read!"

—**Cyril Chappellet**, *Chairman and Chief Executive Officer,* Chappellet Vineyard

"Vikram is among today's greatest independent thinkers and prides himself on being a generalist in a world of specialists. He stands out in the world, and this is his story. It's a fascinating tale of how he went from the son of immigrants to becoming one of the most influential insiders in politics and world affairs."

—**Jim Cantrell**, *Chief Executive Officer,* Phantom Space; *Founding Team,* SpaceX

"Through his unique storytelling approach, Vikram shares lessons learned along his journey to becoming one of the preeminent generalists of our time. And while he admits there is no one way to *become* a generalist, he adeptly describes a generalist *approach* that embraces uncertainty, creative and critical thinking, and respect for perspectives other than our own. In today's either-or world, Vikram offers a both-and mindset. A must read!"

—**Christopher A. Leitner**, *Chief Executive Officer,* Tenaska

"Vikram Mansharamani is a world class thinker, a loyal friend, and a faithful citizen. Vikram's story embodies the American values of fair play, hard work, and self-reliance. Vikram thinks for himself—even when it's hard—and has made a life of helping others do the same. *The Making of a Generalist* is a must read for anyone who wonders what is possible if they dare to resist the pressure to specialize."

—**Worth Wray**, *Geopolitical Analyst, Venture Investor*

"With *The Making of a Generalist,* Vikram has demonstrated once again why he is such an effective business consultant and strategist. His mind works similar to AI in that he sees the big picture and is a master at connecting the dots. His ability to see the macro picture and immediately identify trends and patterns is why he is so successful. In addition, he combines a great deal of common sense and personal empathy with each relationship."

—**W. Grant Gregory**, *Retired Chairman,* Deloitte

"Mansharamani encourages students, colleagues, executives, and readers to think differently. He stresses the importance of challenging the status quo to understand how seemingly insignificant factors come together. His thought-provoking reminder that connecting dots is often as useful as generating them will inspire you to be more curious. A must read!"

—**Alicia Edsen**, *Vice President*, Kiewit Corporation

"A very entertaining introspection (infused with Vikram's unbridled 'joie de vivre') on how to expand one's horizons and gain a greater understanding of, and capacity to contribute to, today's increasingly complex and rapidly changing world."

—**Brigadier General Dana H. Born, USAF (Retired)**; *Lecturer in Public Policy,* Harvard Kennedy School

"From humble beginnings to a leading global thinker of our time, Dr. Mansharamani shares how his lifelong "generalist approach" can help us navigate today's omnipresent uncertainty and serve as a guiding principle to make us more aware, compassionate and kind."

—**Scott A. Draper,** *Partner,* Algert Global

"Specialized experts keep getting big things wrong, because they know too little about how the rest of the world works. *The Making of a Generalist* is an important and timely corrective to the doctrine that we should always defer to the specialists. Vikram Mansharamani equips us to learn from others in unexpected ways."

—**Avik Roy**, *President,* The Foundation for Research on Equal Opportunity; Policy Editor, *Forbes*

"*The Making of a Generalist* shares Vikram's personal story and the many lessons he's learned as a son, father, husband, investor, academic and political candidate. His captivating stories reveal a wealth of insights that can help all of us navigate a chaotic world filled with experts and uncertainty."

—**Kenneth M. Bird EdD**, *President and Chief Executive Officer,* Avenue Scholars

"Vikram tells a clear story that's more important than ever - how hard work, clarity of thought, and practice lead to success. His perspectives are told from his first hand experiences mastering his craft and are so relevant in today's dynamic world."

—**Jeremy Hitchcock**, *Co-Founder,* New North Ventures

"By relentlessly pursuing a life of learning, experience and broad expertise, Vikram has developed a highly refined lens through which to view the world and the great issues of our time. He is indeed an expert at navigating uncertainty. *The Making of a Generalist* is a "how to" manual for aspiring leaders and decision makers, and a testament to Vikram's grit, determination, self reliance and optimism. I only wish I had been exposed to such wisdom much earlier in my life."

—**Mark Hart**, *Chief Investment Officer*, Corriente Advisors

"Vikram's tale of a road less traveled is as inspiring as it is thought provoking. Intermingling his life story with life lessons while doubling down on the value of generalist views in a hyper focused, over specialized world of experts encourages the reader to embrace the world through the widest of lenses."

—**Derek Leathers**, *Chief Executive Officer*, Werner Enterprises

"Vikram's book is wonderfully written, and an important story for anyone to read who doubts the American Dream is still alive today. His journey is truly one of a "fox, an outside the box thinker," resisting the continual pull to focus on that one thing, and thus allowing him to help us see the bigger picture."

—**Robin Wiener**, *President*, Institute for Scrap Recycling Industries

"I've benefited from Vikram's friendship and counsel over many years and am thrilled the world will now have the opportunity to learn from his unbelievable experiences and insights. This book will help you understand why open-minded generalists will have a major impact on the future."

—**Michael Sonnenshein**, *Chief Executive Officer*, Grayscale Investments

"Vikram's journey is inspiring and instructive. He has not only lived the American Dream by seizing opportunities when presented, he's also sought to give back and serve the country he loves. Readers of all ages will enjoy his stories and benefit from the lessons he shares."

—**Jim Grogan**, *Chairman and Founder*, SSOX Global

"*The Making of a Generalist* is a thought-provoking exploration of life, its complexities, and the value of embracing a generalist approach. For readers who seek to chart their own path, free from conventional rules, this book serves as a valuable guide and source of inspiration. Everyone has a life story, and this book might compel you to write your own."

—**Fawwaz Habbal**, *Former Executive Dean of Education and Research*, Harvard John Paulson School of Engineering and Applied Sciences

"With his mosaic background of professional and personal experiences, Vikram Mansharamani shines light on a new mindset for business, culture, and a worldview that combines both purpose and openness. A thinking man who turns ideas into kinetic energy, *The Making of a Generalist* is a must read for anyone looking to challenge themselves to be curious, intellectually honest, and unleash their own potential as an individual in an interconnected world."
—**Matthew R. Bartlett,** *Former Director of Public Affairs and Strategic Communications,* US Department of State

"Vikram's remarkable journey has been filled with rare accomplishments, insightful experiences, and magnetic encounters with giving mentors. The lessons he shares in this hard-to-put-down book convincingly point to the generalist mindset as common sense."
—**Anita Naik Madhav, DDS,** *Owner,* Preston Bend Dental

"As a leading, global voice in money, economics, and finance, Vikram Mansharamani provides multi-dimensional insights around many of today's most important topics and trends. In *The Making of a Generalist,* we learn not only how he became an independent, open-minded thinker but how he fought to be heard and create positive change in conventional academic and professional worlds that failed to value unconventional intelligence and thought-processes."
—**Lori VanDusen,** *Founder and Chief Executive Officer,* LVW Advisors

"Mansharamani's journey is both remarkable and relatable, unconventional and full of lessons we can all learn from. The *Making of a Generalist* is not just about the tradeoffs associated with picking various pathways to pursue. It shows how intellectual curiosity, a growth mindset and a willingness to try and learn from new experiences can enable a rich, broad-based fulfilling life beyond what one might normally expect."
—**Howard Wolk,** *Co-President,* The Cross Country Group

"Another out-of-the-box book by Vikram that makes people ponder the world in new and fresh ways. *The Making of a Generalist* offers great exercises to improve your thinking fitness and mental endurance."
—**Craig Benson,** *Chief Executive Officer,* Planet Fitness

"This book is a real life story of the hope and opportunity that characterize the American Dream. Vikram's journey is personal, heartwarming, and thought provoking. It inspires readers to think about how they can create and seize opportunities for themselves, their families, their businesses, and society as a whole."

—**Fee Stubblefield,** *Founder and Chief Executive Officer,* The Springs Living; *Partner,* Pendleton Beef

"*The Making of a Generalist* is a vibrant tribute to the unconventional path and a must-read for anyone who wants to become a more adaptable, creative, and independent thinker. Mansharamani's unique blend of humor and insight offers a fresh perspective on something we know all too well - the value of being a 'square peg in a world of round holes.'"

—**Christopher Pavese,** *President and Chief Executive Officer,* Broyhill Asset Management

"Most of the simple problems in life have been solved. We are left with many wicked hard problems, that are amazingly complex, and often confounding, with no simple answer. Vikram represents a new way of thinking…to integrate and balance many different opposing issues and perspectives…to become generalists who can see the entire forest, as well as the trees. This highly readable book points the way towards tomorrow's biggest breakthroughs. The future belongs to generalists."

—**Charles Miller,** *Chief Executive Officer,* Lynk Global

THE MAKING OF A
GENERALIST

An Independent Thinker Finds Unconventional
Success in an Uncertain World

Vikram Mansharamani

**OUTFOX
PUBLISHING**

Copyright © 2024 Vikram Mansharamani

All rights reserved. No part of this publication in print or in electronic format may be reproduced, stored in a retrieval system, or transmitted in any form or by any means, electronic, mechanical, photocopying, recording, or otherwise without the prior written permission of the publisher.

The scanning, uploading, and distribution of this book without permission is a theft of the author's intellectual property. Thank you for your support of the author's rights.

Distribution by Bublish
Published by Outfox Publishing, an imprint of Kelan Publishing

ISBN: 979-8-9897304-2-1 (eBook)
ISBN: 979-8-9897304-0-7 (hardcover)
ISBN: 979-8-9897304-1-4 (paperback)

To my parents, Shobha and Vishnu, for recognizing America as a land of opportunity—and for initially tolerating, reluctantly accepting, and ultimately encouraging my wandering ways with great enthusiasm.

To my children, Tori and Kai, may you remain open-minded, curious, and always respectful of perspectives that differ from your own.

To my wife, Kristen, for everything.

Contents

Introduction: A Fox among Hedgehogs xiii

1. The Migrant Mindset 1
2. "Look, Ma, No Hands!" 11
3. "I'll Earn It!" 17
4. Flying Phones and Caring Mentors 23
5. Vinnie Visits Peddie 29
6. Both-And Living 33
7. New? Yes. A Haven? Not Quite 39
8. Illiberal Education 47
9. Talking Grant to Earn Jacksons 53
10. Watch Actions, Not Words 59
11. Practical Wisdom 65
12. Jackass of Many Pursuits 69
13. "To Pay What Is Owed" 75
14. A Pigeon, Castle, and Proposal 83
15. "One of Ours?" 89
16. Rational Irrationality 95
17. A Budding Pracademic 103
18. Insight to Action 109
19. Tossing and Turning 115
20. Academic Bubbles 121
21. A Goddamn Tragedy 125
22. Chain Reactions 131

23. A Professional Thinker 139
24. An Indian among Cowboys 143
25. Does Breadth Trump Depth? 149
26. Foxy Thinking 155
27. Expert after Expert 161
28. Your Latest? 165
29. Escaping Refresh Mania 171
30. Lenses, Loops, and Lags 175
31. Movies and Novels? 181
32. Tori Leads the Way 187
33. The Kai Guy Show 195
34. Why Live Anywhere Else? 203
35. Coin of the Realm 209
36. Retail Politics 101 215
37. Two Ears, One Mouth 221
38. Multidimensional Thinking 229

Conclusion: The Journey Is the Answer 235
Acknowledgments 241

Introduction
A Fox among Hedgehogs

People are always trying to categorize and label things—even other people, right? It's quick and easy. Professionally, we're lawyers, doctors, teachers, farmers, accountants, mechanics, and so forth. Academically, we're either gifted, average, or challenged. We have this degree or that degree. We're educated or dropouts. Politically, we're either Republicans or Democrats. We're labeled by our skin color, our heritage, our religion, our age, our body shape, our sexual orientation, and on and on and on. If you don't fit neatly into this or that box, then you might be a misfit like me—and that's just fine.

Think about it: Can we humans really be reduced to a few small categories? Do *you* fit neatly into a couple of boxes? How about the people you care about—do you typically describe them with a simple label or two? Of course not. Even those who are experts at one thing have wider experiences and broader knowledge to share. All of us are many things—and sometimes, none of the above. By very definition, individuals are unique entities within an indivisible whole. For humans, our personal blends of DNA, upbringing, mindset, and experience contribute to a shared heritage as *Homo sapiens*. And as peculiar vessels of knowledge, information, and wisdom, no two members of our species are alike. Isn't that amazing and wonderful?

Somehow, though, in today's polarized world of siloed, either-or thinking, we seem to have forgotten that this amazing cacophony of diverse perspectives and ideas is a gift perfectly suited for our increasingly complex problems—and it's not a gift we can afford to squander right now. So why do we continue to regard each other with the limited vocabulary of labels, boxes, and silos? I know I don't fit easily into a box, and you shouldn't have to, either. The world needs each of us and all of us to share and consider each other's full range of perspectives and ideas. In an era defined by polarization, it's time to start listening with open hearts and minds again instead of dismissing each other as this or that. We need to think for ourselves, respect each other, and move beyond labels and boxes. Not doing so is destructive. With authentic curiosity, we must explore many viewpoints and regularly challenge our own beliefs. It's the only way to start thinking more holistically and critically *together*. Less either-or thinking, more both-and collaboration. The combination will help us successfully navigate the uncertainty and challenges of the twenty-first century.

This is why the only label I'm willing to accept is the one I've created for myself, mostly to appease those who still want to label me. I proudly call myself a generalist with a capital *G*. Russian-British philosopher Isaiah Berlin might have called me a fox among hedgehogs. Berlin wrote about the difference between these two animals in a 1953 essay, basing his ideas on a parable by the ancient Greek poet Archilochus: "The fox knows many things, but the hedgehog knows one big thing."

Those of you who have read my work before will have heard this analogy. But for those new to my story, here's an overview: Though different, foxes and hedgehogs have plenty in common. For one thing, they both exist in an uncertain world, just like we do. The fox responds to uncertainty by learning many things quickly to survive. It lives in a state of constant adaptation and creative problem-solving. The hedgehog approaches uncertainty with a single, important adaptation: self-defense. When it rolls into a tight ball and extrudes its coat of spines, it's difficult for predators to hurt it.

As Philip Tetlock has explained, foxes and hedgehogs help us understand two cognitive styles: "Foxes have different strategies for different problems. They are comfortable with nuance; they can live with contradictions. Hedgehogs, on the other hand, focus on the big picture. They reduce every problem to one organizing principle." Foxes are generalists, and hedgehogs are specialists. Both species have survived for millions of years, so their contrasting approaches both deserve consideration. But which is more equipped to navigate the world's current uncertainties?

To ensure I'm not falling into either-or thinking here, let me clarify: this is not an exercise in foxes *versus* hedgehogs. I am a fox who learns from many hedgehogs. I just think the world needs more foxes because hedgehogs are abundant—and foxes are rare. Society is great at funneling people into areas of expertise but not so good at nurturing generalists. Businesses and academia almost always favor deep expertise and specialization. It's one reason why I've been swimming against the current most of my life. But it has been worth it because I think we all benefit from the unique perspective of the generalists. Here's an example to get you thinking about this: We can certainly agree that expert nuclear physicists help us understand how protons and neutrons combine to form atomic energy, right? This is a necessary specialization. But when it comes to the threat of nuclear war, which is one outcome of atomic energy, the input of many different specialists is required—nuclear physicists, political leaders, economists, watchdog groups, policymakers, country experts, and so forth. Also necessary are the insights of generalists who can synthesize these expert viewpoints and make connections that the specialists might miss. We have plenty of the former and a dearth of the latter.

Despite this imbalance, somewhere along my delightful, sometimes challenging, and usually fulfilling journey, I discovered that being a fox, a generalist in all walks of life, was the perfect job for me—and the way I wanted to live.

It's far from the easiest road, but it has certainly been interesting and, I daresay, fulfilling. I have met with heads of state in

Africa, academics in Lebanon, journalists in India, casino operators in Macau, doctors in Bangkok, cosmetics manufacturers in Russia, miners in Zimbabwe, financiers in Peru, and peace negotiators in Colombia. I've been on safari, gone diving with great whites, flown a helicopter, narrowly escaped an angry mob in Jakarta, played polo in Argentina, drunk too much during a state of emergency in Karachi, and become a regular rodeo attendee. I've had polygraph tests, dodged bullets, and narrowly escaped exposure to Ebola. I've run the Boston Marathon, written three books, and been listed as one of the one hundred most powerful people in global finance. I've traveled by private plane, railcar (with livestock!), and cargo boat, and even sped through the streets of Vietnam on a motorcycle. I have a PhD from MIT and a commercial truck driving certificate from Roadmaster Drivers School, and I've taught at Harvard and Yale. I've eaten Rocky Mountain oysters in Nebraska and *gou rou* in Tianjin, China; been stuck in a sandstorm; had my phone electronically jammed by terrorists in Lebanon; and run for the US Senate in New Hampshire.

What connects all these disparate events? A refusal to let society's expectations guide my actions and a conscious decision to see the world as the extraordinary, interconnected whole it is rather than focusing merely on a fragment or two. It's the interplay between different ideas, viewpoints, and areas of study that excites me. It's jumping from bucket to bucket to bucket nonstop that keeps my thinking muscles in shape and leads me to aha moments that experts often miss. I'm okay being a square peg in a world of round holes. I've found my happy place in our uncertain universe.

My amazing parents, who risked everything to begin a new life in a land that promised unlimited opportunity, taught me that courtesy and empathy should be more than actions; they must be a way of being. Through my family and an eclectic mix of life experiences, I've come to understand and respect that every perspective is biased, incomplete, and therefore limited. And since that's the case, I know my own lens on the world is also biased, incomplete, and limited. So why not adopt multiple perspectives as part of my quest to understand our planet and its inhabitants better? Why not balance rugged individualism with the input of skilled experts? Why not think independently and unconventionally by keeping experts on tap, not on top? This approach has dramatically changed my thinking and the way I interact with the world. It has shifted my relationship with knowledge and the experiences and people who hold that knowledge. Being a generalist keeps me endlessly curious and forever humble—a healthy combination in unsteady times.

Perhaps the most wonderful thing about being a generalist is understanding that while there is absolutely a discernible, definable, perfectible way of *being* a generalist, there is never (ever, ever) a prescribed way of *becoming* a generalist. There are no college majors or degrees, no specific career paths or professional titles, and no self-help books to show you how.

This is precisely why I have chosen to share my life story.

If, like me, you find yourself a square peg in a world of round holes, I hope my journey encourages you to stay strong, forge your own path forward, and remain true to yourself—despite the uphill battles you're sure to face. It may not be the easiest road, but it's very fulfilling and fabulously interesting. A generalist's journey is never boring. I've chosen to share some of the pivotal points along *my* path to becoming a fully conscious generalist. Though your journey will be different—precisely because it will be *yours*—I hope reading about the skills, habits, mindset, and practices I've learned along the way will smooth the road ahead for you. At the very least, I want you to know that you are not alone and that your efforts are worthwhile. For me, pushing through the challenges has yielded rich rewards—opening many doors; presenting many career opportunities; improving my health; leading me to become a better husband, father, and member of my community; and instilling in me an ethos to give back and providing a means to do so.

In a complex and uncertain world full of hedgehogs, more foxes—more confident, conscious generalists—could help address today's intricate global threats and challenges. We foxes are still a scarce breed, even though, at the end of the day, I believe we are all capable of being both specialists and generalists. And because we are lucky enough to live in a country that encourages freedom of thought, expression, and speech, we have a constitutional right to debate; dissent; and form strong opinions, ideas, and perspectives. This should never be taken for granted. With these inalienable rights comes the responsibility to listen to and respect the ideas of our fellow Americans—even when we disagree with them. Because the more either-or thinking we do, the more labels we apply and use to dismiss opposing viewpoints, the less vibrant our democracy becomes. America's great tapestry of ideas should be celebrated and cultivated.

If you don't want to be put in a box, don't put others there. I've been fighting against this type of behavior my entire life. Instead, be a fox, an outside-the-box thinker. I've been on the generalist's journey since I was a child, even if I didn't know it all those years ago. It has been a long, winding, uphill road with fascinating scenery around every corner. I've had my fair share of challenges, laughs, tears, and moments of immense joy along the way. I hope you'll find my story interesting and useful. In the end, the most important thing I've learned is that the generalist's journey is never-ending—so, *festina lente*! Make haste slowly. Your journey awaits.

CHAPTER 1

THE MIGRANT MINDSET

My values were shaped by my parents. I am the son of two hardworking immigrants. Seeking better, they followed the rules that welcomed them to the United States, then followed the rules that made them citizens of the United States. They embraced the promise of America and contributed what they could. Like countless immigrants turned citizens and their firstborn American children, my life wasn't a straight, obvious, or predictable path. It was, however, consistently instructive. One of the more important lessons I learned as a child was this: how you behave on the journey matters more than your often-unknowable destination. It's your behavior that creates not only opportunity but also joy, meaning, and purpose.

Like all children, I didn't reflect much on any of the habits of my home or neighborhood. Tuesdays followed Mondays, weekends followed weekdays, and we all did our best to cope with the twists and turns of daily life. Only much later, after understanding uncertainty became my profession, did I go back and think about how lucky an inheritance I'd had.

My parents gifted me a "migrant mindset." The concept of an "*immigrant* mindset" is well established and often associated with risk-taking and entrepreneurialism. Some have defined it as an enabler of innovation, a catalyst for fresh thinking. The *migrant* mindset, on the other hand, goes well beyond this idea. Immigrants go from point A to point B in hopes of better; migrants move with agility among many points in pursuit of better. In other words, the immigrant mindset is either-or thinking, and the migrant mindset is a both-and approach.

Within and outside of career and professional settings, the migrant mindset encourages movement across silos, classes, and cultures. It embraces existing knowledge while seeking advantage from hubs of knowledge everywhere. Though I learned about the migrant mindset through my experiences as a first-generation American, this way of thinking is readily available to anyone. All of us, at some point, encounter the core tenets of the migrant mindset. In a community approach to embracing the full potential of the individual, you (a) contribute when possible, (b) respect others who know more than you might, and (c) understand that there is always more to learn. Whether cross-town, cross-continent, or cross-oceans, migrants leave much behind when they seek better. But importantly, they bring along what they know and how they know. In my childhood home, the latter included the explicit injunction to "do your part," which, as a child, often boiled down to being both a good guest and a good host, perhaps my earliest exposure to the power of silo-crossing, generalist living.

Good guests are respectful of their hosts. You don't impose what you know—your worldview, your traditions, your particular knowledge—on others. You remain curious and open to the experiences you are having, and you contribute wherever and however you can. A good guest is thinking about her host and wondering, *How can I help? I should clean up after myself. What are the rules of the house, and how do I abide by them?* And also, I should think, *What can I bring to this party to make it better? To your empanadas, let me bring my naan.* The main thing is bedrock common courtesy, to think about the needs of those who are opening their home up to you.

And the same goes for being a good host. Good hosts think about how to make their guests comfortable. It's about respecting that others may be less aware of or less comfortable with your traditions and that there is something to be gained from the empathy of trying to place yourself in another's shoes. The key lesson, of course, is that at all times, we are all both guests and hosts.

Crossing silos, eschewing either-or framing, and adopting multiple perspectives—all tenets of foxy thinking—are quintessentially American, I have come to learn. The United States is a country that fervently embraces a distinctive balancing of responsibilities and rights, collective and individual efforts, freedoms and civic duties. A nation of people who came from elsewhere, yes, but what defines us, I believe, is a shared heritage of values and virtues echoed in institutions and law . . . but also cemented in a pattern of behavior, a mindset. The **migrant mindset**. No one better exemplifies this mindset and all it can accomplish than Alexander Hamilton, who went from immigrant to revolutionary to secretary of the treasury and was among our most influential Founding Fathers.

THE PURSUIT OF BETTER

My father arrived in America in the mid-1960s as a student seeking an automotive technical education. Armed with an associate of applied science degree that he had earned in India in 1957, he enrolled in Roberts' Technical and Trade Schools in Manhattan and began his journey toward acquiring a skill, some know-how, that might enable a better life. Unsurprisingly, there were struggles along the way. He ran out of tuition money. To secure room and board, he lived in a hotel and worked as the overnight front-desk clerk. He made money driving a cab. Throughout it all, he never wavered. He knew America was where he wanted to stay, where he intended to set down roots.

After his stint in Manhattan and now armed with his technical certification from Roberts, a job, and a green card, he returned to India to inform his family that America was going to become his home. When he returned to the United States, this time married, he settled in Queens, New York, among that borough's large community of immigrants from the Indian subcontinent. Finding a cultural network in a new country can be very helpful to immigrants. But for my dad, it was always a beachhead to something grander, not an enclave within which to preserve things left behind. He wasn't content in Queens. He hadn't left India to remain so exclusively among his fellow expatriates. Immigrant, yes, but his migrant mindset made him aware that there was far, far more to America than Queens, including, not insignificantly, towns of green grass, open spaces, and more varied neighbors. And that is where he took his young family when I was nearly five years old.

The choice of rural-suburban Landing, New Jersey, can obscure the fact that my dad is guided by a real spirit of adventure. To a man who had navigated Bombay (Mumbai) as a child, some of the roughest parts of West Africa as a young adult, and then Manhattan and Queens as a budding professional, Landing, a town of just a few thousand, was another thoughtful roll of the dice. Later in life, I learned it was useful to think of people on a spectrum between explorers and exploiters. Explorers take risks and try new things. Exploiters, on the other hand, thrive within what already exists, using (sometimes using up) what they find there. On that spectrum, my father was definitely an explorer.

He was born outside of Karachi in 1937, in what was then part of British-occupied India. In 1947, when he was just over ten years old, his life was upended after the British left and India was partitioned into independent India and Pakistan, which resulted in the Hindus of Pakistan being exiled from their homes. As my father later noted in his journal, "Every day, there were riots, looting, murders and beatings/killings in the streets . . . so one evening, we all walked to the seaport where cargo ships were taking Hindus to India." For the next few days, my young father lived on a few slices of bread (on occasion with butter or jam) and was eventually deposited in Bombay. His journal continues: "We stayed in tents for a couple of weeks" before his family was able to secure employment and begin life anew.

A few years later, after a bit of formal education in India, his adventurous spirit drove him to West Africa, where he secured an opportunity to work with Indian entrepreneurs involved in the automotive business. As his journal notes, "I was offered a job (which I had found through a local Sindhi newspaper) in Freetown, Sierra Leone, as an auto parts salesman. The conditions were as follows: a 2- to 2.5-year commitment, salary sent to your parents in rupees monthly, and you'll be provided lodging, boarding, and all necessary requirements, including to and fro airfares to be paid by the company."

My father recalls Freetown as not very comfortable: "No tar roads, limited running water, occasional electricity . . .

no TV, radio for a limited time each day." Given that, it is unsurprising that he also recalled, "We all used to drink a lot every evening." After some time, he was transferred to the Gold Coast, known today as Ghana. After finishing that contract, he returned to India to see family before seeking another contract in Africa. He noted, "This time, luckily, I was asked to go to Lagos, Nigeria . . . where I was happy. Lagos is more advanced than Freetown and Accra. Most of the people in Nigeria were educated, cultured, and good-mannered." Despite the calls from colleagues to drink every evening, my father enrolled in a correspondent's course at the British Institute of Engineering Technology: "It kept me busy from evening to midnight and all day and nights on the weekends." He earned a certificate in automobile engineering during his eighteen-month stint in Lagos before returning to India again. While at home with family, my father proposed Hong Kong as the destination for his next work adventure. His parents did not approve—Hong Kong seemed too distant, too foreign—so he returned to Nigeria.

Which is where he listened to stories about America.

After hearing of a country in which your status was determined by your efforts, where anything was possible for anyone, and where protections in law and property assured the fruits of success were enjoyed by those who created them, my father simply had to learn more. He went to the US embassy in Lagos and gathered all the brochures and papers that were available. He remembered one that had a profound influence on him: "How to Study in America with Little Funds." America was seductive. He simply had to find a way to get there. After applying to several schools, he recalls, "I got a favourable reply from Roberts Technical and Trade School on 57th Street [in] New York—it said admission was available every six months, including student visa guaranteed if enrolled." He broke his contract with his employer, reclaimed his passport, and delivered all documentation to the US embassy in Lagos. Within a week, he had what he today calls the golden ticket: a student visa to come to the United States.

Upon reaching America, he knew his life as an immigrant was over. He had landed on the shores of a country he wished to make his home. However, he also understood that his years as a migrant pursuing ever-better opportunities would continue. Both understandings were soon reflected in his becoming an American citizen, something he recalls with fondness and pride.

My parents' decision to leave the immigrant community in Queens, New York, for Landing, New Jersey, fit my father's pattern of deliberative exploration. Needless to say, names like Mansharamani were not very common in a small New Jersey town of a few thousand people. But he was undaunted by the challenge of creating a new life for himself and his family in a strange new place—which, for me, of course, it wasn't. Though I was born in Queens, all of my earliest memories are from the garden parts of the Garden State. This, for me, was home.

We were a novelty, and not. We ate different food. My parents had barely noticeable foreign accents. But we lived in a house that, from the outside, looked like everyone else's. Our neighbors' names, just like ours, spoke of migrations, perhaps farther back in time, from England, Poland, China, Italy, Ireland. The town's landscape of places of worship did the same; we lived among Jews and Catholics and Presbyterians and Episcopalians. One friend's mother had the best lasagna, another's had prized empanadas, and another's had corned beef, and we all had boxed cereals, Chips Ahoy! cookies, and rarer, Hostess snack cakes. Sure, my family's daal and naan were outliers, but not wildly so. Just as our being lower middle class was an outlier, but not wildly so. Even when my dad's gas station was doing its best and we moved to a bigger house—more bedrooms and, importantly, more bathrooms—our living room had no furniture. This wasn't a reflection of a cultural tradition but a consequence of strained budgets.

Childhood in the Mansharamani house was not carefree. My father was an auto mechanic by training, a service manager, and briefly a small-business owner. He bought, ran, and lost to bankruptcy a gas station with two service bays. My mother was a dietitian, commuting back and forth to a regional hospital. There, as a requirement of employment, she was a member of the health-care workers union. And the union provided her a community that helped her both navigate employment within a large organization and discover relationships, commonalities, and shared interests. Both busy, my parents watched my sister and me grow up in suburban New Jersey, often by proxy, as a wider community of neighbors, teachers, friends, and fellow immigrants chipped in to protect our collective well-being. And my parents chipped in whenever possible as well. I remember carpooling to preschool with my then-classmate Eric Sinoway and remember my mother picking up both of us after school and taking us to various parks. (Interestingly, Eric was the best man at my wedding and remains one of my closest friends today!) With the arrival of my sister, Vanita, who was born ten years after me, I was even more on my own as family came together to help with the newborn and, later, toddler.

So when I wasn't outside with the neighboring kids, I spent a lot of time watching sitcoms after I finished my chores and homework—what could be more American in the 1980s than that? From *The Brady Bunch* to *The Jeffersons*, my predinner downtime was consumed by what five channels of television offered. We also stayed in contact with the Indian community in Jersey, driving for hours on weekends to spend time with extended family and friends. Like our kitchen pantry, life was a mash-up of traditions and tastes discovered and strengthened day over day. My father and mother made clear, however, that this was what it meant to learn, adopt, and adapt. It was what it meant to be American.

CHAPTER 2

"Look, Ma, No Hands!"

As a kid, what I learned about being an American—at home, at my neighbors' homes, at school, among my community—was straightforward, if not always simple. It was both-and that my father exemplified: *both* guest *and* host. Perhaps some of this came from his experiences moving from Karachi to Mumbai to present-day Ghana and Nigeria and then the US. He was used to being a guest. And of course, once settled into a community, he often wanted to reciprocate and, in doing so, became a host. As mentioned earlier, the reality is that we are all both guests and hosts in the dance called life.

We can all intuitively understand these roles, and every culture has strong traditions respecting hospitality, about being a good guest, and about being a responsible host. The story behind America's great secular holiday, Thanksgiving, after all, is a celebration of hospitality, of the lifesaving cooperation between hosts and guests. Like the migrant mindset, courtesy within community is a national habit, a reciprocal promise of good intentions and behavior. The United States has historically been very successful at being host to immigrants.

No country comes through history unblemished, of course, and exactly when the label *immigrant* dissolves—in one generation? two? five?—is murky and, ultimately, unhelpful. I believe a better approach is through some new language to get at an older truth:

America has historically been welcoming of explorers. Not perfect, but the diversity of the cultures in the country is a testament to its ever-renewing spirit of generosity in sharing the opportunities America offers with those who are willing to be both good guests and good hosts.

I was making the most of my own opportunities at my middle school in Mount Arlington, where kids from Landing were sent. I was a good student and did well in my academic classes, but the first assignment I can remember being proud of was for shop class. I chose to make a toolbox, which involved drafting a schematic, folding metal, cutting wood with a bandsaw, sanding the sides and handle, and then staining the smooth wood. Amazingly, in the end, it actually resembled a toolbox! I had made something! And what's more, I gave it to my father, who filled it with the tools he used to fix cars. It was great! It showed me that with time, patience, the right tools, and a sufficiently skilled teacher, you can make something that is functionally useful.

This was the beginning of my love of invention—first of things, then of ideas—but always with the aspiration of their being functionally valuable. Usefulness became a guiding light.

So when I heard of a contest open to school kids inviting them to create inventions to solve practical problems, I was in. It was known as the Mini-Invention Innovation Team (MIIT) contest, and it was a statewide competition. My shop teacher at the time, Mr. Worobetz, encouraged my entire class to compete, and many of us did. The inventions were to be judged at the school level, and if they were deemed good enough, they would progress to regional and state competitions.

The question my thirteen-year-old self came up with wasn't "What might win?" but "What practical problems did I have?" Getting in and out of the shower came to mind. I was always annoyed with fiddling around with the shampoo bottles and soap. This wasn't as inconsequential as you might think. At the time, our house had one full bath, and shower time was precious, along with hot water. (And of course, you didn't want to be in the shower if someone flushed the other toilet, which made taking a shower something that demanded the utmost efficiency!) What, I thought, if I could make the soaps and conditioner mix into the water before it left the showerhead? A "hands-free" shower? This was my concept, and using some of the fabricating savvy I'd acquired in shop class, I set about making it a reality.

My presentation consisted of a piece of wood, about three or four feet tall, two inches wide, and two inches thick, that was attached to a base. I put tile on the wood to make it resemble a shower wall, and on the top, I attached a showerhead. Three pumping soap dispensers—the kind you might see in a gym shower—were attached by tubes to the pipe that fed water to the showerhead. The idea was that when you pumped the dispensers—one each for shampoo, conditioner, and body soap—the contents flowed directly into the water as it made its way into the showerhead. Voila, soapy water, hands-free!

This concept and the working prototype I'd made were good enough to get me invited to the regional competition, but there, things would get trickier. Judges would now be interested in whether I understood the science behind my invention and whether scientific principles could be applied to make it work. I needed help. I needed expertise. And I remain eternally grateful to Mrs. Buffett, my science teacher, who supplemented the tactical skills I was acquiring from Mr. Worobetz.

She was my seventh-grade science teacher at Mount Arlington Public School and one of the most influential educators in my life. Not only was she inspirational, caring, and supportive, but she was a crucial figure in my early intellectual development. She encouraged her students to think beyond the memorization and regurgitation of facts in textbooks. She wanted us to think for ourselves about the underlying concepts we were learning and applying. It was the extension of the concept of guest and host into the realm of knowledge and education. In Mrs. Buffett's class, you brought what you knew to what she knew, and your slow mastery of the latter was the triumph.

When it came time to break down the science behind my hands-free shower, Mrs. Buffett was the one who guided me to Bernoulli's principle.

Daniel Bernoulli was an eighteenth-century Swiss physicist and mathematician who first worked out important mathematical models for how fluids behaved. Applied to my experimental shower invention, Bernoulli's principle predicts that if water is moving fast enough through a pipe past a hole of the correct size, a vacuum is created such that whatever is on the other side of that hole—like, say, soap—it is going to get sucked into the passing water. I remember standing in the yard of my house with a garden hose, experimenting with water pressure and hole sizes to get something that would work. Eventually, I did. Today, Bernoulli's groundbreaking work is fundamental to understanding some of the most important inventions in modern life: how carburetors function in internal combustion engines and how the shape of airplane wings produces lift. Now, courtesy of an assist from Mrs. Buffett, I could add my hands-free shower to the list!

I won the regional competition and was on to the New Jersey statewide competition, to be held at Georgian Court University and judged by Princeton University professors and other scientifically accomplished luminaries. Each competitor had his or her own booth, and judges walked around the room, booth to booth, examining the different inventions. By that point, I had not only refined the mechanism of my invention but also my pitch, which was printed on the posterboard behind me. Here's a sample of my Barnumesque copy:

> Have you ever had the feeling of being upset about not being able to get the cover off the shampoo, conditioner, or liquid body soap? Maybe you've been upset about not being able to reach a spot on your back with the soap. Well, your problems are now over. My new idea is a new and revolutionary concept that will put an end to your problems and troubles.

The Making of a Generalist

Okay, it wasn't great language, but I was thirteen years old. And the description of my experiment was more matter-of-fact: "The concept will have three bottles mounted on tiles behind the shower. These three bottles will have tubes leading from them to the water tube. Timer release buttons control the flow of shampoo, body soap. It is easily connected to a shower with a simple connector. The simple connector requires two threaded things." A diagram made clear that by this, I meant small nozzles from which tubes would run. "The other attachment is connected to the showerhead. It only costs a few dollars to make. This product is revolutionary and will turn anyone into a clean person."

The judges may not have agreed it was "revolutionary," but they thought it was good enough to win among the other 4,200 participants. And just like that, I was the state champion of invention. If you dig up old copies of the June 18, 1987, edition of the *North Jersey Advance*, you can find a picture of me, at thirteen years old, in an ill-fitting tie and shirt, standing next to my contraption under a headline that reads "Look Ma, No Hands!" The September 11, 1987, edition of *India Abroad* also ran a story about me, "13-Year-Old Inventor Is Honored," and many in the Indian American community reached out to my parents with congratulatory notes.

I was a minor celebrity. Even some lawyers saw the article, and not long after my success was announced in the papers, I was approached by several men offering to get me a patent for my invention. After we found out that this would cost $800, my father nixed the idea, thinking it was a fraud. Perhaps. On my own, I wrote to several companies seeking sponsorship, but my letters either went ignored or met slight encouragement: "A good idea, but it's never been done." Years later, when I google "hands-free shower," however, I see numerous claimants to the invention.

At the time, though, I couldn't have cared less. The best part of winning the invention contest was one of the prizes: a guided tour of Princeton University's plasma physics lab. I was allowed to invite one adult to accompany me, and that was Mrs. Buffett. We got to see some mind-blowing stuff—cutting-edge fusion experiments performed with the most advanced equipment and facilities that made clear the gap between Mount Arlington Public School and a top-tier college. I was overwhelmed by it in a way that lingered.

My success with the invention contest opened new opportunities for me—and new aspirations. Suddenly, going to a college like Princeton didn't seem impossible—after all, at thirteen, I was already rubbing shoulders with members of its prestigious physics department. But Roxbury High School, the regional high school that would be my destination upon graduation from Mount Arlington, did not have a great track record for placing students in top colleges and universities. Sure, some students had gone on to great success, but most did not. And it had larger classes. It also suffered from some of the sad difficulties that plagued American education—I recall hearing about kids with drug problems and more than one bomb threat. It was toward the end of my middle school years when I learned there were other options. I was talking to a classmate who told me he was leaving public school to go to a private school called Morristown Beard. *Can I go to Morristown Beard?* I wondered. Not lost on me was the fact that the classmate with whom I had this first conversation was known to be from the wealthiest family in our small community.

CHAPTER 3

"I'LL EARN IT!"

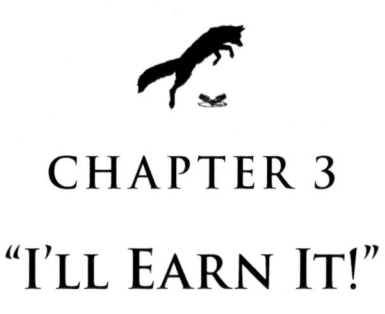

Then I heard about Blair Academy. A guidance counselor knew of my inquiries about other educational options, and she was also aware that my family lacked the financial resources for me to attend a private school. She passed along an announcement for a scholarship at a private school. Not Morristown Beard, but Blair. She helped me fill out the application, I submitted it, and after a wait, I learned that I had secured a scholarship covering 50 percent of the expenses. I was ecstatic. My parents, however, were more realistic: "That's great—congratulations. But where will the other fifty percent come from?"

I was undeterred. My initial response was "I'll earn it!" Heck, I had turned a few bucks into a winning invention that, along with the trip to Princeton, earned me a $250 savings bond. Digging into the math, however, quickly removed this thought from my head. At this point, I realized that Jack Bogle, the donor behind the scholarship, must be a wealthy man. *If he's willing to support 50 percent,* I thought, *perhaps he'll support more.* How to find out? Well, I tried sending a message to Jack Bogle, founder and chief executive of the Vanguard Group and inventor of the index fund. While I waited for a response, my parents agreed to accompany me on a tour of Blair, during which time they made clear that the generous scholarship was, for my family, just not generous enough. Upon learning of my interest and my family circumstances, the response was quick, and Blair Academy secured another Bogle Brothers scholar.

The summer before I went to private school, I secured a job at the local Wendy's—it was my attempt to earn some cash to help pay for Blair. I also knew that going to private school required some extra dollars for things like books. Because at places like Blair, you *buy* books. Private schools don't reissue old textbooks and ask students to wrap brown paper bags around them to protect them, like I was used to doing at Mount Arlington. Private schools expect their students to purchase brand-new copies of the most recent editions of textbooks. But that was a cost passed along to its students.

Before I could begin my job at Wendy's, however, I had to get special working papers from Mount Arlington Public School to flip burgers at the age of fourteen. The law stipulated that to apply for a job, I had to seek an exception guaranteeing that I would work only outside of school hours and with parental approval. This wasn't that big of a deal for my working-class neighborhood or my family. If anything, the surprise was that we needed to get the school's sign-off. After all, my father had worked in a store as a clerk when he was fourteen. As it happened, the school didn't bat an eye. So, at fourteen, I was in uniform, behind a counter, working the food line and cash register through the morning and afternoon rushes and the lulls in between. I'm proud to say I was the employee of the month in August of that year. I remember it distinctly: a framed photograph of me was up on the wall.

Needless to say, going from employee of the month at Wendy's to a highly competitive private school that today costs tens of thousands of dollars a year was a bit daunting. I knew there would be a wealth gap between most of the other students and me. After all, nearly all of them came from families that hadn't needed to make the case for an even more generous scholarship. Most of them came from families more than able to foot the entire cost of attending Blair, often for more than one child. I distinctly remember when we pulled up in our family car, a VW Rabbit with over a hundred thousand miles on the odometer, how others looked at me slightly differently.

At fourteen, I had a bare appreciation for two facts: One, nothing could have fully prepared me for the wealth disparities I encountered at Blair. It wasn't just among the students; it was immediately visible in the school's facilities. Blair was nothing like Mount Arlington or Roxbury. The other fact was how little it mattered. For starters, there were not a lot of things boarders could do off campus (Blairstown is not exactly a bustling city), so all of us enjoyed and took advantage of the same facilities. And because of the school's dress code, all boys wore more or less the same attire: pants, a button-down shirt, and on occasion, a blue blazer and tie. Crossing campus between classes and sitting in the classrooms, it appeared as what it was—an even playing field. During the semesters, it was easy to imagine that everyone was on somewhat even terms. It wasn't until spring break during my freshman year that I awoke to how big the differences really were.

For starters, spring break ran two weeks, not the one-week break I had at public school. That meant more time to fill, which, I quickly learned, meant exotic travel for many classmates. "I'm going down to Cayman with my family," one said. "I'm heading to Paris," said another. A few were flying to Colorado to go skiing. I chimed in with, "I'm going to Landing, New Jersey. Anyone else going there?"

To the school's and my classmates' lasting credit, no one made much of the differences that, on occasion, were glaringly obvious. And school-sponsored opportunities were open to all, which meant that I wasn't always excluded from exciting spring trips. My sophomore year, I joined a group, led by Dr. Marty Miller, the head of Blair's history program, that went to what was then Czechoslovakia. Marty was fascinating and inspirational. I don't think I've ever met a person who was in touch with a more eclectic network of individuals—poets in eastern Europe, former military guys from Latin America, and historians in and out of academies. He had started a club at Blair called the Society of Skeptics, and though I hadn't taken a class with him, I joined. And I got to know Marty through the random lectures the society hosted. I didn't know it at the time, but Marty was the epitome of a global generalist and became a role model who planted the seeds of what grew into my broad interests in history, geopolitics, and global economics.

At the time he conceived of the trip, the Iron Curtain had only recently fallen. No matter—Marty had a plan: "Let's go to Czechoslovakia. Let's go to Prague." When he brought the idea to me, my response was immediate: "Sure. Sign me up!" Though I didn't really have the money, Blair had extra resources to help a student on scholarship go along on these sorts of trips. So while a bunch of my classmates went to the Cayman Islands or skied in the Alps, I pieced together some of my scholarship funds and a little bit of leftover burger-flipping money still in savings and headed off to Prague. It was awesome. We were chaperoned—Marty had invited a couple of parents to come along, including the parents of friends—so we weren't utterly on our own. Except, to an extent, we were. It was in České Budějovice that I had my first beer. I was sixteen years old, and the good people of Budějovice didn't care. At a pub, we were informed that "this is the home of Budweiser." Caught between the currents of host and guest, and no small amount of curiosity, I said, "Okay, great!"

It was my very first visit to Europe, and it was amazing. I had enough presence of mind to think I might have caught echoes of my dad's earlier exploring. Marty also made the experience better than it might otherwise have been, imbuing life into history and sharing his passion beyond the classroom. He never allowed any students to lose sight of the importance of also going out and rubbing elbows with that wider world they were reading about. Spending time with Marty taught me that adopting a migrant mindset generated a deeper understanding of the changes happening around the world.

Academically, I hit my stride the moment I arrived on Blair's campus. I was not an athlete, however, and Blair insisted that all students participate in sports. I had played soccer in the Mount Arlington town league and kickball and other gym sports in my public school, but my parents weren't jocks and had little to no time for events and travel teams. Once I learned that participation on a team for at least two seasons was required at Blair, I had no idea what to do. I figured I was okay at tennis, so that got spring covered. What about another sport?

First, I tried wrestling. That lasted less than a week. It wasn't just a gut reaction of "What the heck have I gotten myself into? No way, not for me." It was also the fact that I'd stumbled into a bastion of highly accomplished expertise. Wrestling was the best sport at Blair. To this day, the Blair wrestling team competes around the world, and it has produced multiple Olympians. My gut instincts were right: nope, not for me!

Which is why I turned to swimming, which proved to be a marvelous experience. I was no more gifted at the sport than I had been at wrestling, but the path to a personal best was visible from the start. First, the coaches who ran the program, Rick Clarke and Bob Brandwood, were unbelievably encouraging and firm at the same time. They knew how to manage the delicate balance of pushing student athletes to excel while at the same time remaining supportive. For me, that mattered.

I came to Blair as an out-of-shape, overweight ninth grader. The snacks and television showed, as well as my comp meals at Wendy's. Bob and Rick didn't care. The opposite. They encouraged me to keep with it and not measure myself against my teammates. Amazingly, my peers followed their lead, and the result was a real compete-against-yourself dynamic. In fact, one of my closest friends from my time at Blair, Chris Passannante, was breaking most of the school and pool records both on campus and around the state. And he was also among the most encouraging of peers, alongside fellow swimmers Jonas McDavit, Susan Dana, and Molly Bracken. Nevertheless, my objective was clear. By my senior year, I was going to swim the hundred-yard freestyle in under a minute.

I never achieved it.

Though I failed at that specific objective, I consider my swimming career a success. I started out with the unremarkable time of over two minutes for the hundred-yard freestyle. I ended up with a time of 1:02, which, for me, was impressive. More important, however, was that Bob and Rick wouldn't even hear of defining what I'd accomplished as anything other than a triumph, even though I never won any races. An overweight kid had gone into that pool, and a healthy, in-shape kid had, four years later, come out of it.

My entire four years at Blair were characterized by friends and mentors who took me for what I was and what I could contribute. In return, I was presented with opportunities they and the school made possible. When I left Mount Arlington for Blair at fourteen, I had essentially moved away from home. I was a boarding student, wet behind the ears but eager to learn about all aspects of the world I was becoming an adult in. I recall one year being asked by then-headmaster Jim Kelley to address the school's trustees. I did, and coached by some of the administrators, I decided to end by declaring a personal ambition.

The problem was, I had too many. Invent and innovate, travel, read and learn broadly, come to see and understand the world in ways Marty and others had introduced me to. On which ambition should I conclude? I knew enough about the trustees, however, to understand that "I'm curious about everything" wasn't right.

Having glanced at a few of their biographies, I ended my address with "I'd love to explore a career in finance or economics." It felt like a cop-out. I should have been honest: truth be told, I had no idea why I needed to focus on one domain. The pressure to appear "focused" was overwhelming, and it would take some time before I had the courage to push back.

CHAPTER 4

FLYING PHONES AND CARING MENTORS

By my junior year, I was looking for better summer employment than my old Wendy's job, so I again wrote to Jack Bogle, who had taken an interest in me, to see if he had any internships available. I was curious to follow up on my naive curiosity in investing and knew enough to understand that Bogle seemed the right go-to guy. I asked him if there were any opportunities at Vanguard. He promptly replied, "Ah, Vikram, you don't want to come here. We don't do anything here. We do passive investing—we just literally outsource everything."

I was confused. "What's passive investing? It sounds like it's investing. That's what I want to learn."

He didn't miss a beat. "Nah, it's not what you want to do. Tell you what. Call up this Blair alum Mitch Jennings, who is a pretty senior guy at Bear Stearns. That's where you want to go." So I set up a time to speak with Mitch, and after a five-minute call, he offered me an internship and told me to come to the office when I was ready to start.

"When?"

"Whenever—next week, next month."

I showed up in early June 1991. The commute was not easy. First, my father or mother had to drop me off at the Dover, New

Jersey, bus terminal, which was about thirty minutes from our home. There, I took a bus to the Port Authority Terminal at 42nd Street and 8th Avenue, a trip that would add an hour. I was then in a part of Midtown Manhattan that was still pretty rough by New York City standards, but in the late 1980s and early 1990s, before Times Square was revitalized and turned into a family-friendly destination, it was notorious for being a center of prostitution, pornographic movie theaters, and drugs.

In my ill-fitting jacket and tie, I walked through it all to get to 245 Park Avenue, the global headquarters of Bear Stearns, a legendary Wall Street firm. But as I soon learned, it wasn't the only building where Bear Stearns had operations. On my first day, I was assigned to the Stock Records Department, which was figuratively and literally located far from the shiny and glamorous Midtown offices. Stock Records occupied a dark, dank, and hidden-away building in Brooklyn. To my trek from my home in Landing to Dover by car, then Dover to the Port Authority Terminal by bus, I now added a subway ride from Port Authority to Brooklyn. It was two and a half hours each way, every day. And I said, "That's fine. This is what I want. I am here to learn."

My job was to physically move stock certificates. That's what Stock Records was all about. The department managed the physical paper that represented shares in America's largest companies. It was menial, albeit important, clerical work. After that commute, I probably nodded off three times on my first day on the job. And it was only after doing this *for a week* that I spoke with someone who asked, "Are you sure there's not something else they can give you to do? It sounds like they're happy to have you do anything. Maybe there's something else, somewhere else. Maybe something back in headquarters?" But I didn't want to make waves and stuck with moving stocks. Finally, one of my teachers at Blair told me that I should at least tell Mitch how things were going. A few days later, I called him and left a voicemail telling him that I was working in Stock Records and that I was really grateful for the job.

Mitch's response was, "You're doing what?"

The next day, I was on the institutional equity trading floor, which is one of the most desired placements for any intern anywhere on Wall Street. And I was assigned to work directly for the head of US institutional sales, Ricky Greenfield, a kind and supportive man who seemed to take an interest in my experience. He placed me in the middle of the action. I got a front-row seat on IPOs. I got to visit the research floor. I saw Bear Stearns taking companies public, taking them private. I learned of mergers and acquisitions and boardroom battles. I was having lunch in the executive dining room even though I still looked like a scholarship kid who didn't know any better—dressed in a poorly tied tie and a discount jacket. It's embarrassing in retrospect. But I met with consistent, if brusque, kindness. In fact, someone looked me up and down and said, "Maybe we get you some clothes. Something that fits." And they did.

Sartorial anxiety aside, it was an awesome experience. I was seeing a whole new world. Dollars were flying everywhere. There were days you not only had the sense of being at the epicenter of world events, but in fact, you were. I ended up splitting my time between institutional sales and trading and research. That matters. The departments were kept on different floors. And historically, there's a Chinese wall between them. If research is going to issue a new report urging people to buy this stock and sell that one, federal law requires that this not get to the trading group ahead of it getting to the public. And I, the summer intern, fluidly worked between both groups, with no one ever taking advantage of the fact. What also became clear was that Ricky Greenfield was hardly alone in taking me under his wing.

One day I was walking the research floor, and someone threw a phone at me. That's what they did during that particular stretch of Wall Street's history. Put it down to the frenetic pace of the work. But when someone throws a phone at you, you do the next obvious thing. For me, that meant pick it up, look around, and lock eyes with its owner.

"Kid, who's your sponsor?"

I missed a beat. "Sponsor? What do you mean?"

He replied, "A kid like you doesn't get a job here unless you have someone senior looking out for you. Who's your sponsor?"

"The guy who hired me is Mitch."

"Mitch Jennings?"

"Yeah."

Now he didn't miss a beat. "Ah, kid, let me take you out to lunch."

That is how I met Chris Bodnar, who became an early mentor and friend. At the time, Chris was a young equity research analyst covering chemical stocks. He included me in research. He took me out to lunches and introduced me to a bunch of people in sales and trading. That was in 1991, my junior year at Blair. I remember watching the Japanese bubble burst and people going crazy. The Nikkei had hit nearly 40,000 before it started cratering. Everyone was wondering, "What the heck is going on?" So began my interest in financial bubbles, which are not just a financial curiosity but can drive the broader economy. When the Nikkei burst, a few traders seemed to think that bubble was going to drive the global economy off a cliff.

In addition to Chris and Ricky, there were a bunch of senior Bear Stearns folks who took the time to help me out. The Wall Street I entered was not the cutthroat, dog-eat-dog world I had imagined. While it may have been that for others, I was probably disarmingly naive, innocent, and therefore respectful. The migrant mindset that my parents had gifted me, which had served me well in Czechoslovakia and Blairstown, it turns out, was just as useful on Wall Street.

On the trading floor, several people went out of their way to help me learn about the world I had entered. Bill Finn, a gentleman through and through, would often take out a notepad and explain basic bond math; he taught me concepts such as P/E ratios and dividend yields. I often wondered why he cared enough to teach me and once asked him. His response was as telling as any about the value of the migrant mindset: "I cared because you cared. You asked questions; you didn't pretend; you were genuinely interested and curious." The admiration was mutual, and while I kept him abreast of my final year at Blair, then my years at Yale and beyond, he sent me a sweater almost every Christmas until he passed.

Another mentor and friend was Maureen Sherry. A tall, athletic, and gorgeous woman who had graduated from Cornell, Maureen was kind enough to invite me to roadshow presentations over fancy lunches. (A roadshow, I learned, was when a company ran around Wall Street and told their story in the hopes of convincing investors to buy their stock.) When one presentation was canceled, she offered to take me out to lunch anyway. She suggested sushi, at which point I likely grew bright red and started sweating through my shirt. You see, I had never tried sushi, and with a family from poor regions of India, the idea of eating something raw was scary. Maureen noticed my discomfort and offered to help me overcome my fear. "If you're going to be on Wall Street, you're going to be exposed to sushi," she said. She and two of her colleagues, Jill and Amber, who had also been kind and supportive of me, then took me to a sushi restaurant and proceeded to order one of every type of fish on the menu—both to teach me and to allow me to sample every kind. Maureen became a mentor, friend, and even a source of financing when I made my first stock investment!

Then there was Marie Lugano, a feisty New York woman who ran events for the sales team. She was amazing. Organized, diligent, and firm. I listened to her negotiate with the best and win. And while other interns focused on sales, trading, and other aspects of investment banking, I was curious as to what she did and asked lots of questions. Like my relationship with Bill Finn, it was filled with mutual respect and admiration. She later went on to found the American Menopause Foundation and even assisted my mother with navigating some health matters. Right up until her death in 2022, she made sure to call me every year on my birthday to check on me and my family and hear about the ups and downs of life.

Ricky, however, was a mentor of mentors. An unbelievable guy who was a source of support and encouragement for decades till he passed away. He exemplified the extreme of common courtesy, when you deliberately reach out and help someone overcome one of life's tough, transitionary spots because you can, because it is the right thing to do. When I finished my senior-year internship, he bought me a laptop for college. He paid for it, handed it to me, and said simply, "When you go to college, you should have a computer." That night on the bus ride home, I was in tears—of joy, of course.

CHAPTER 5

VINNIE VISITS PEDDIE

By my senior year at Blair, I knew I belonged. No, I had no illusion that I was one of the Cayman Island–Aspen set, and nor did they. Rather, among the people I cared about and who cared about me, it was understood that my family's finances didn't matter. I was who I was—a swimmer who had gone from horrible to not bad, a student who had gone from good to really good, and a contributor to the Blair community. I was thinking of ways to give back when the school was gearing up for its annual rivalry football game against another New Jersey prep school, the Peddie School. They had been competing with—and pranking—each other since 1903.

That was when I had a eureka moment somewhat akin to my hands-free shower. In this case my inspiration wasn't for a physical invention but for a mischievous, slow-burning practical joke. I had been reading about lampoons and satire and studying the genre with my English teacher and mentor, Andy Hays. I had been skimming *Punch* magazine, had read about the annual MIT pranks during the Harvard–Yale game, and was fascinated by the creativity involved in successfully executing satire. I was appointed the editor in chief of the school's literary magazine, *Between the Lines*, during my junior year. On Valentine's Day of that year, we produced a satirical version of our own magazine and called it *Between the Sheets*; it featured lampoon-ish stories about on-campus romance. Fellow swimmer and friend Jonas McDavit and I also led a group of like-minded pranksters to lampoon the school's newspaper, the *Blair Breeze*. For the cover story of that issue, we asked headmaster Chan Hardwick to pen a serious article about illicit drugs. He obliged, and we ran it as the lampoon's cover story with a picture of him and a headline that read "Hardwick on Drugs."

These efforts had inspired me, but I was now thinking bigger, and I wanted a capstone senior-year spoof. So I suggested to Jonas, my partner in these efforts and the truest of friends, and Andy Hays, the faculty member who oversaw the literary magazine and school newspaper, "Let's do a satirical prank against Peddie." They didn't miss a beat: "Sure, what do you want to do?"

We outlined our vision and immediately jumped in without hesitation. Andy, Jonas, and I (and several other students) got together and, armed with a copy of the rival school's newspaper, the *Peddie News*, figured out its layout and style. Then, I called up the Peddie School admissions office and pretended to be a New Jersey public high school student considering a postgraduate (PG) year to better prepare for college. I told them, "Hey, I want to come. I'm thinking about a PG year." I gave my name as "Vinnie Spitoli," a tribute to the character played by Sean Penn in *Fast Times at Ridgemont High*, and played Vinnie up like he was a member of the Soprano family.

Peddie set up a time for me to visit the campus and interview. On the day of the appointment, I put on a gray suit, black T-shirt, and three or four big gold chains. I borrowed a car from my parents and drove to the campus. I brought a camera and armed myself with a couple of impressive facts about Peddie to show that I had done some diligence.

After talking with the admissions officer, Vinnie Spitoli then got a tour of the campus, all documented with my trusty camera. I got to visit the locker rooms, where I got pictures of freshman football players holding jerseys. I had the admissions director and his assistant smile for me on campus. I also took a picture of the main gate, which had "The Peddie School" mounted upon it.

Armed with all these pictures of Vinnie visiting Peddie, we went back to Blair's student newspaper offices and began to put together our alternate *Peddie News*. The week before the big game, we finished it, and with some extra money Andy scraped together, we printed a thousand copies and delivered them to the Hightstown campus for the entire Peddie community to read. Our mock version, complete with pictures of Vinnie on campus, an article about the admissions director (accompanied by a picture of him grinning), and a story about the football team (among many other stories), was a hit. We even doctored (this was before Photoshop) the main gate to read "The Annenberg School" after the school's main benefactor.

That wasn't all. Vinnie himself arrived at the big game, blinged out in his gray suit and chains, sitting in the back of a convertible (driven by none other than Chris Passannante), where Vinnie—or, now that the joke was obvious, I—was treated like a minor celebrity. It all worked. People took pictures with Vinnie, and everyone had a laugh.

There is an important coda to this story, one that gets to the heart of not just a rivalry but my time at Blair and the world of Blair–Peddie. That fall, while I was applying to colleges, I had a thought. Why not ask the Peddie admissions officer who offered Vinnie a PG year for a recommendation letter to round out my application to Yale? I asked, and he not only said yes but gave me a copy.

"I'm going to share what I said so that you don't worry." His letter was forthright. He couldn't comment on my academic abilities or grades since I had attended another school. What he could say was that I was creative and had an "ability to empathize and make people comfortable." He told the full story of Vinnie, adding, "I was a victim of it, but it was all in good fun." He attached to his letter a copy of the fake *Peddie News*, which became a part of my official application to Yale and every other school to which I applied.

In thinking about my college choice, I had applied to the usual suspects for a high achiever coming from a private school: Princeton, Yale, MIT, Harvard, and so on. But like many choices for me at this stage of life, the ultimate decision was based on financial considerations. Yale offered the best financial aid package, which would put less of a burden on my family. I was New Haven–bound.

I didn't appreciate it at the time, but my playacting as Vinnie Spitoli would be a fitting capstone to my life up through my graduation from Blair. For years, I had benefited from transparently being both-and. A child of Indian immigrants growing up in a quintessential small American town. Both the statewide winner of an innovation contest and a flipper of burgers. A son of blue-collar workers and a student at Blair Academy. A scholarship kid and an intern on Bear Stearns' research floor, both Vikram Mansharamani and Vinnie Spitoli. Over all of those years, I migrated among people and places that wondered, first and foremost, what I brought to an opportunity and then judged me by how I behaved in pursuit of it.

Why would Yale be any different?

CHAPTER 6

BOTH-AND LIVING

Without ever having to think very deeply about it, I grew up knowing that there were generalists among us. From parents and neighbors to Mrs. Buffett to Dr. Miller, from my swimming coaches to Ricky Greenfield, from Blair to Peddie, I'd encountered guests and hosts, mentors and experts, generalists and specialists. Indeed, I grew up assuming everyone was a generalist first, specialist second. Every adult I encountered had an occupation, but they also gardened, fiddled with tools to make various home repairs, and engaged as members of the community in social or service groups. Surely, this made everyone a generalist first, right? My personal experiences further validated this sense.

For example, working a fast-food counter or pumping gas demands a generalist's talents. If you have never worked either job, then the truth of that might escape you. Sure, taking orders chosen from a limited menu or removing a cap and inserting a nozzle before releasing the flow of gas are among the most monotonous, narrowly repetitious of occupations. But that's only seeing the task from one side of the exchange. Having worked both jobs, I can tell you that successfully dealing with a steady stream of customers from all walks of life requires a nimble and attentive mind.

During my breaks from school, I pumped gas at my dad's station. New Jersey, in its infinite wisdom, made it a law that an attendant must fill your car's tank—no self-service anywhere from High Point to Cape May. Early on, I learned that this job was both tedious and demanding. Each customer presented a small universe of unique possibilities and needs. You met their eyes. You listened to their tone of voice. You matched patience with patience, impatience with professionalism. And you learned to make no assumptions. Often, it was the mother of three driving the decade-old station wagon who tipped and the solitary suited professional in the leased Mercedes who wouldn't even return a hello. Just like when I worked the Wendy's counter, I needed to be both mechanical and adaptive. Most important, every customer served represented a brief interaction of both host and guest, a situation in which I was, unknowingly at the time, practicing the migrant mindset.

What made these interactions with customers easy for me was that they distilled everything I'd learned throughout my childhood. Before I ever graduated from Blair, before I ever gained acceptance to Yale, I had enjoyed years of experience with the importance of both-and. Both guest and host; both Landing, New Jersey, and Blair Academy; both gas station attendant and Bear Stearns intern. It was so instinctive; I didn't give it a thought. My young adulthood through age eighteen was a prolonged window of time during which balancing many demands, such as home, school, work, and internships, and multiple worlds—Landing, Blair, Bear Stearns—was just another week, in another month, in another year.

In the late spring of 1992, I graduated from Blair at the top of my class. When I had arrived four years earlier, I was initially hesitant about this new world I was entering. You don't go from a rural New Jersey public middle school to the campus of Blair without immediately understanding a "before" and an "after." I knew from the outset that Blair promised a better education than might otherwise have been available to me. But I wasn't naive. I knew I was going to stand out from most Blair students.

That was unavoidable. My skin was slightly darker, my last name unpronounceable. I also presumed that being a full-scholarship student would mark me as different, despite the school's best efforts to keep such information hidden from the community. The concern that all of this would matter to Blair or its students—on that I was mostly wrong. Sure, I had to work summer jobs, and my family didn't take vacations, but no part of Blair, from athletics to academics, was off-limits. My teachers expected just as much from me as they did from my peers. And not once was I treated, by students or faculty, as anything other than just another student. That I could do more for the school paper than the swim team was obvious, as was the fact that I did my best at both.

The same dynamic had played out at Bear Stearns. I was given the opportunity to work hard. I had, and with it came more opportunities. The exact same was offered and expected of every intern, and most of us competed to demonstrate that we deserved each opportunity.

By the time I was throwing my mortarboard up in the air upon graduation from Blair, I firmly believed that having navigated private school and my internship at Bear Stearns, I had earned my place in New Haven at the starting line of adulthood. I assumed the same dynamic would be present at Yale—every student was both individually different and part of the same incoming class.

If anything, I figured I had an advantage. I was long familiar with the world of both-and, both different from and genuinely deserving. If I lacked the material resources of other students at Yale, the same had been true at Blair. What I had instead was the blessing and support of my parents and the examples they had set for me. And a growing cadre of supportive mentors and friends.

Always with me was my father, a refugee turned explorer of Africa before making his way to the United States. Always with me was my mother, who had uprooted herself from India to join my dad in the exploration of the United States, from the familiar Indian enclave in Queens to rural New Jersey. They both worked tirelessly at demanding jobs to make better lives for themselves and their kids. Lesser but essential parts had been played by Susan

Buffett, Jack Bogle, Mitch Jennings, Rick Clarke, Bob Brandwood, Marty Miller, Andy Hays, Maureen Sherry, Chris Bodnar, and Ricky Greenfield. Also essential was a vast cast of individuals whose names I never knew, from Wendy's customers to New Jersey mass transit bus drivers.

At nineteen, I appreciated all of them. Uppermost in my mind, however, was an awareness of my parents. Their sacrifices had created my earliest opportunities, and I had done my best to live up to what they had made sure was available to me. At the time, none of this seemed remarkable. That is what parents do, right? And it's what mentors, at school and places of employment, do. Sure, parents lace it with love, and employer mentors lace it with expectations, but the reciprocity is similar, to both help and be helped. There were times when I knew there were more enjoyable things I could do than pump gas for Dad, but there was never a time when I wouldn't say, "Yes, I'll help," when he asked me. Similarly, I both moved stock certificates in a warehouse and supported research sales on the trading floor.

By the time I was packing for my first year at Yale, having just completed a second summer interning on Wall Street, I understood explicitly the ethic of being guest and host and implicitly of living both-and. My admission to the university was *both* the result of my taking whatever natural talents I had *and* exercising them under the guidance of others. I had *both* busted my butt for years *and* remained open to what came my way, whether at the gas station or traveling with Blair to Prague. I clearly understood my young life to be one spent grabbing at an opportunity, making the most of it, and having some fun along the way. Yale, one of the nation's preeminent institutions of learning, would be no different, or so I thought. Armed with my migrant mindset, I was confident I'd be able to both contribute to and also learn from the community of scholars.

What I didn't think at the time was that my early success, or that of my parents, was an example of the "American Dream." Growing up, I don't remember a single conversation about how we were pursuing or living our lives according to any such dream. We

The Making of a Generalist

were too busy living those lives, in fact. These included setbacks—none greater than my father's loss of his service garage and gas station—and then our house, to bad timing and bankruptcy. We, and our extended family, owned the setbacks as much as we owned the successes. I assumed this was just normal life. Learning how to better navigate life's uncertainties, I assumed, was the point of Yale.

It just made common sense. Attend Yale, earn the vantage point of a first-rate education, and then be positioned to continue the pursuit of better. Yale would be Blair, only grander. Or so I expected.

CHAPTER 7

NEW? YES. A HAVEN? NOT QUITE.

Yale marked the beginning of my decades-long exploration of the skills and demands involved in living as a deliberative and professional generalist. Not coincidentally, it was at Yale, as I marched toward my twenties, when I first encountered the numerous forces that pushed me toward specialization.

I distinctly recall arriving at my assigned residential college, Silliman. Yale has a residential college system into which its undergraduates are divided among, at that time, twelve "colleges." Silliman, appropriately on College Street, would serve as my home on campus for the next four years. That first day was a scene of utter chaos. Out of a wide variety of cars spilled students, suitcases, and boxes. I noticed not only varied skin colors but even different languages being spoken. I was quickly introduced to the dean of Silliman College, Hugh Flick, an academic who had a PhD in Sanskrit, a fact that enabled him to bond quickly with my parents. Almost as quickly, I met my roommate, Steve Guyer, a churchgoing Midwesterner who had earned a spot on the Yale football team.

My first twenty-four hours at Yale met my expectations of it being an enclave of competitive smarts, where a diversity of ideas would be reasoned and debated among people of different backgrounds.

The sifting and sorting of students would be based on the quality of their expressed ideas. At Blair, success—such as pranking Peddie—could be both individual and communal. At Bear Stearns, top performers were obvious by their track record and valued accordingly. At Yale, once again, I assumed students would be measured by individual and communal achievements and assessed by performance.

By my second day on campus, I began to have doubts. I soon discovered that wider cultural wars raged inside the walls of this ivory tower, and propaganda and passionate anger were all too often driving the conversation.

When I think about the cultural conflicts that existed below the sedate surface of college life in the early 1990s, I'm reminded of a moment I observed on that second day. Two students, a man and a woman, were approaching the front gate of Silliman College. The man grabbed the handle of the gate and, with a chivalrous flourish, opened it for the young woman. She stopped and, casting him a withering glare, said, "I can open the door for myself, thank you!"

The whole interaction made no sense to me. Why had a simple, courteous act—the kind of thing the world could always use more of—been rebuffed, and in such harsh terms? Behind the counter at Wendy's, I had dealt equally with the rude and the kind, and the latter left me grateful. At Yale, why was courtesy complicated? It was as if the simple give-and-take of guest and host had gone out the window. Whether in my Irish or Philippine friends' homes in Mount Arlington or the restaurants of České Budějovice, the instinct upon encountering something different was to ask politely, "What's that? May I try some?" And whether that was followed by "interesting" or "delicious," no matter what, you said, "Thank you so much!"

As I met more and more of my classmates and began interacting with older students and members of the faculty, it seemed that a surprisingly large number of them wanted to find reasons to feel aggrieved. Every action or utterance could be interpreted in the worst light, as evidence of a hidden intolerance. As a first-generation American, I couldn't wrap my head around it. Sure, America had its flaws, but so, too, did every other nation. But America was a land of opportunity, that shining city on the hill that drew my dad and millions like him to come to its shores. America was a work in progress, always improving. America was, in all its glory, a process—not an outcome.

Precisely because I knew the world of lower-middle-class options, two-parent working homes, and mixed immigrant neighborhoods, when I encountered the focus on America's lapses of its founding principles, I understood how important it was to seek evidence of the *opposite* being true. I'd just spent eighteen years living a life of earned opportunity and progress. Far from encountering systemic barriers, my path to Yale had been carved by my repeatedly stepping into transparent tolerance.

Why were so many of my college classmates, who were enjoying the privilege of a luxurious Ivy League education, so angry?

One answer to this question became clear to me, and with the benefit of hindsight, it is finally beginning to make sense today: students were being encouraged to think of themselves as victims in a nation beset by reasons to feel aggrieved. It was the opposite of being both different from and deservedly the same. However, having arrived in New Haven, all of us together made up Yale's class of 1996, right? Well, not exactly. The system celebrated differences rather than fostering commonalities. You weren't ever just a Yale undergraduate; you were a Yale undergraduate with particular qualifiers, more often than not with characteristics that served as reasons for aggrievement or stigma.

Even more confusing, in the eyes of some percentage of Yale, I was expected to be living proof of these aggrievements. Like most colleges, Yale had a variety of orientation programs for first-year students. One of the popular ones was called FOOT, the Freshmen Outdoor Orientation Trip. In this program, older students led first-years on short, guided hiking trips into the wilds of Connecticut. On the hikes, students could bond with each other and learn about what they might encounter in college. I was eager to participate in one of these trips.

Sadly, it soon became clear that campus administrators had other expectations of me. You see, there was another orientation program, designed specifically for minority students, called the Pre-Registration Orientation Program (PROP). It was created in the early 1970s to help students from Puerto Rico adjust to the cultural and academic challenges they were presumed to face at Yale. This was also around the time that Yale and many other universities began lowering admissions standards for minority students to increase the racial diversity of their student bodies. Over the years, PROP had expanded to include students who had been born and raised in the United States but stood out, usually just because of the color of their skin or the number of vowels in their last names. PROP was intended to make it easier to integrate students into Yale. In practice, the entering minority students funneled into PROP were separated from most of their classmates during the early weeks of college, when many long-lasting friendships are formed. Rather than unifying the incoming class, this program began dividing it at the very time when it was essential not to separate students by identity. And this was among the earliest signs of the hypocrisy and counterproductivity that characterized much of this supposed do-gooding.

But there was a deeper, more hurtful quality implicit in PROP. It intentionally denied that I, or a whole range of students, could be both-and. Because we were in some way categorized as a minority, we could not be handled as every other Yale undergraduate. We could not be both different and equally deserving. That most fundamental generalization—every incoming freshman was in this experience together—was being turned on its head.

I didn't want special treatment, and I didn't want to be cut off from most of my peers. I wanted to do what most other Yale students were doing. So, to the chagrin of one of the deans, I opted for the regular orientation after a much-abbreviated participation in the minority one.

"But you won't get the *full* PROP experience," he told me. "We will give you extra support. There's tutoring and counseling and other things to help you."

I was deeply offended. I had been the valedictorian of my senior class. I had academically outperformed all the other students at Blair, many of whom had also gone to highly selective colleges. I also had great standardized test scores and had worked demanding summer jobs. Hell, at thirteen, I had been a statewide champion inventor! I had done a bunch of cool things, maybe even more than some of those now hiking the hills of Connecticut. But all Yale could see was the color of my skin, the length of my last name, and the scholarship that spoke to my family's socioeconomic standing, so the presumption was that I needed special treatment if I was going to succeed. Far from being a solution to a problem, this seemed like the invention of a problem.

I have no quarrel with the idea that some incoming undergraduates might benefit from a program such as PROP. But to impose it on all minorities struck me as the very opposite of America's many stirring evocations of equality, arguably the most memorable being Martin Luther King Jr.'s "I Have a Dream" speech. It is a vision that is anathema to default categorizing. During my four years at Yale, I encountered students who needed additional help, a percentage of whom were descended from the Puritans or third-generation legacy Yalies. Surely the point of PROP, now more blandly titled Cultural Connections, was that Yale would provide help to anyone needing it? After all, we were all classmates, weren't we?

How the university went about offering help instilled the opposite belief. The casual assumption that everyone lumped into this amorphous group—"minority student"—needed access to special services was not only condescending to students, but it also fostered separatism, which is the opposite of what an orientation program for college students should be doing. Students, it was implied, were either this or that, but surely not both this and that. Why did one have to live in only one box? Not for the last time, the attempts by the administration experts at Yale, however well intended, to direct my decision-making were met by me with an emphatic "No, thank you."

Most nonsensical to me was the experience of Yale wanting it both ways. It wanted to declare to the world and its students and alums that it was a meritocratic institution that collected the best of the best and helped them prepare for rich, fulfilling, purposeful lives. And it wanted some of its students and alums to understand that it was making amends for past wrongs. To redress its history of exclusion, it would carve out separate places for the newly included, re-creating and strengthening the very ailment it sought to cure.

This was the very opposite of both-and thinking. Programs like PROP telegraphed to the world that undergraduates were *either* attending Yale based on merit *or* to atone for the university's history of discrimination. PROP ignored the fact that undergraduates could be *both* minority scholarship recipients *and* accomplished students who had earned their spot at Yale. It introduced entire freshman classes to the idea that you could, at a glance, distinguish true "Yale material" from those who were somehow inherently less deserving of a spot at such a coveted university. PROP was the university's feeble attempt to address past mistakes—but it backfired. Instead of an ethos that students of differing and unique backgrounds were equally deserving of the shared opportunities offered to all Yale undergraduates, the program seemed to suggest some students had faced less rigorous admissions standards because of their background. Mind you, none of this was ever explicitly stated, but the feeling that being part of PROP was a negative label was pervasive. I felt it, as did many of my peers.

It made no sense. Worse, it was self-defeating.

Even then, I knew that if admission standards are relaxed for some categories of people, anyone in these categories is liable to be stereotyped. To Yale's legacy problem—for decades, it had lowered standards for children of alums and the privileged—it had added a social stigma problem: to balance legacy students, it would lower standards for the athletically gifted and the culturally different. Why did extending the same bad past behavior to even new categories of students make sense? Why not open the door to whomever Yale elects to admit; let them in; and let the admitted sort themselves out by effort, ability, and that mix of luck and risk that is life? Frankly, the same meritocratic spirit of opportunity for all that made America great could and should characterize university education—not only at "elite" schools but all schools.

CHAPTER 8

ILLIBERAL EDUCATION

Perhaps the most insidious consequence of Yale's focus on difference is that once this type of thinking is introduced, we can all prove susceptible to it, as I learned not long after I started my freshman year. I soon noticed that I had been infected.

I remember walking into the dining room with my roommate, Steve Guyer. He and I had bonded quickly. My summers working fast food in Jersey and interning in Manhattan meshed easily with his high school football career in Painesville, Ohio. I marveled at his Midwest as much as he marveled at my Mid-Atlantic. Steve continues to be one of my closest friends. To people obsessed with race or culture, we must have seemed like an odd couple, but really, we had a lot in common. Like me, he came from a family of humble, hardworking parents, and we each felt a little out of place in this highfalutin New England university.

After we grabbed our food, Steve and I went looking for a place to sit among the sea of new faces. That's when we noticed an enormous guy at one of the tables. Steve was a pretty big guy, but this guy was monstrous—maybe 6'6" and 300 pounds, 250 of it pure muscle. I immediately thought, perhaps a little dismissively, *Oh, he must be a recruited athlete.* So, I believe, did Steve. Since Steve had been recruited for the football team, he didn't hesitate to put his tray down and start talking to the guy. To our surprise, we discovered that this giant had not been recruited for football at all. Athletics had been, for him, an afterthought. In response to Steve's queries, he replied, "I might go try out, but I'm not sure."

As it turned out, Nick Adamo was just a brilliant student and a hard worker who happened to look like he could be in the NFL. For me, this freshman-year meeting shattered the idea that I should judge anyone by appearance. I had been in New Haven for mere days and was already falling into the habits of the very administrators I had pushed back against. Thereafter, it was repeatedly confirmed that policies that treat people differently based on superficial assessments—however well intentioned—are wrongheaded.

Nick ended up becoming one of my best friends in college. In the end, he did join the football team, as a walk-on, and he did really well. As with Steve, he and I had more in common than you might imagine. Nick also felt out of place at Yale. He also had a work-study job—he worked in the dining halls, whereas I worked in the library—and he was also from New Jersey, so my parents would sometimes give him a ride home on holidays. As I got to know him, I found out that my first impressions of him were even more off base than I realized. After we became good friends, he confided in me that at times when he was growing up, he and his father had been homeless, sometimes living out of a car. There were times when they weren't sure where their next meals would come from. And somehow, against these enormous odds, he had made it to Yale.

Along with trying to figure out where we fit and alongside whom (and often doing so against the interference of the school's administration), there was the schoolwork itself. In this domain, Yale lived up to my expectations. Though not perfectly, academics did sift and sort students. It could be daunting, but it was invariably helpful.

I arrived at Yale with the goal of studying physics and art. I'm not exactly sure why I chose these subjects, beyond a desire to exercise both the right and left sides of my brain. I remember telling parents and administrators that my goal was to get a broad and comprehensive education. That was a way of conveying, in terms I thought people would accept, that even then, I knew the blinkered, focused path of a single straight line to a lifetime career as a doctor or lawyer wasn't appealing. So I plunged into the deep end, registering for Physics 260, a course that would not only set me on the path toward a bachelor of science degree and a master's degree in the subject at the end of my four years but would also position me, the inventor of the hands-free shower, for a lifetime of profitable patents.

Within days, I realized I was in way over my head. I sat through the first few physics lectures lost, not understanding a word the professor said. The math was beyond me. The theory of relativity, which I thought I understood, suddenly seemed incomprehensible. I was drowning. Recently, I looked at my old notebooks from that class, and the most common symbols on the pages aren't Greek letters from a mathematics equation but question marks. I had filled page after page with question mark after question mark.

On top of this, Physics 260 required lab work, which meant we had to meet up in the afternoons. For the art student in me, it was torture to be in the labs, setting up oscilloscopes and multimeters, on a beautiful fall day. I had trouble focusing. It didn't take me long to see that absent intervention, I was destined to fail the class.

For a moment, I even doubted myself. Maybe I should've gone to PROP?

Fortunately, I found a different, better solution: John Meeks. He was a sophomore in the same class and a friend. John was not only truly brilliant, but he was also deeply empathetic and generous toward this poor freshman who was obviously out of his depth.

He broke down the course for me. "All right," he told me one day, "you're not going to get an A in this class. But if you want to get a C, here's what you can do." He helped me understand the math and concepts that were within my grasp, guided me through the lab assignments, and lent support when I faltered. And sure enough, I was able to pull off a C. It is the only grade that wasn't an A during my entire time at Yale, and it sits at the very top of my transcript. And while John may not take pride in helping a friend get a C, I can honestly say he was a godsend, and his generosity saved my freshman fall.

Though it was the lowest mark I received at Yale, it is one of the ones I'm proudest of. My physics teacher had been talented, fair, and mostly unhelpful. The decision to take Physics 260 had been a mistake, my mistake. Acting out of courteous courage, John took me under his wing and helped me plot a way not to drop the class but to complete it. There was more honor in that outcome than any other.

It was one among many lessons I learned that fall. At the same time as I was grinding my way through physics, I was also taking an introductory English class. It was a pleasure. I was stepping into the black eye my transcript would take in physics. I was determined to make up for it elsewhere, starting with that English class.

During the final examination period, I stayed up late to prep for questions on Chaucer's *Canterbury Tales*. It was to be my very first final exam, not only of the period but of my Yale career. It was past 2:00 a.m. before I went to bed. The exam was set for 9:00 a.m., which meant I'd get a little sleep before grabbing a shower, breakfast, or maybe just coffee. The next morning, I woke up and looked at the clock, and to my horror, I saw that it read 10:30 a.m. Even though it was winter in New Haven, I instantly broke out into a sweat. I ran to the examination room and arrived as students were filing out.

The professor, a man named Fred Robinson, saw my panic as I apologized and explained to him what had happened. "Don't worry about it, Vikram," he told me. "Take a shower, have some lunch, and meet me at the Elizabethan Club this afternoon for tea."

I went home, gathered myself together, and then went to the club. Professor Robinson couldn't have been kinder or more gracious. He asked me to recite some of the lines from the prologue, and we discussed my impressions of Chaucer and his work. Then, and I could scarcely believe it, he told me, "This is fine. The exam is a requirement—I'm forced to give them. But I just want students to learn. Consider this your examination. I hope you have a wonderful Yale career."

I was stunned. My first exam at Yale was a conversation over tea at a private club in New Haven. It made a huge impression on me as a kid from a lower-middle-class family from New Jersey. Not the private club, not the tea, not even the graciousness of this older Yale faculty member. Compared to PROP, it made sense.

Throughout that English class, I had distinguished myself, done the work, done it well, shown up on time and prepared for each class, and consistently proved my love and dedication to the subject. Unquestionably, when it came time for the exam, I had stumbled. The late night, the alarm, the bed, the whatever: I had slept through the final. What mattered to my professor, however, was evidence of achievement.

It was another odd moment in my young life as I continued to straddle the worlds of my background and the strange new culture I was encountering, first at Blair, then Bear Stearns, then Yale. The governing ethos of Blair—show us what you are capable of—extended even to its archrival, the Peddie School. At Bear Stearns, that I arrived by way of a two-and-a-half-hour bus ride, walking through streets riddled with drugs and pornography, and started my first summer internship filing stock certificates never kept me from eventually being invited to eat in the executive dining room. The governing logic was both fairness and accomplishment. The guiding question wasn't "What do we owe you?" but rather "What can you help make happen?"

CHAPTER 9

TALKING GRANT TO EARN JACKSONS

No surprise, but when my first semester at Yale ended, I decided that a physics major wasn't for me. So, for my spring semester, I decided to throw myself in the opposite direction. Instead of hard science classes, I decided I'd try something in the social sciences. That's when I fell in love with political philosophy. It was the study of questions I'd long been interested in and loved to debate. How should societies be organized? Who deserves what? What is the role of government? How do we make society more equitable, just, and rewarding? Blair had given me a rudimentary exposure to philosophy, but now I was immersed in a serious way in the ideas of Hobbes, Locke, Rousseau, Mill, Burke, and Marx. It was thrilling. I realized that these men hadn't wrestled with abstract, inconsequential concepts but with vital ideas forged in the political conflicts of recent centuries. Ideas that continue to define the shape of our political debates and institutions today.

As the spring went on, I began to think about what I would do for work when the school year ended. Returning to Bear Stearns for a third summer seemed like the logical choice. I called up Ricky Greenfield to ask him if he'd take me back. Everyone I knew at Yale seemed to be trying to get jobs on Wall Street, so I felt especially lucky to have an inside track. Not only had I already worked there for two summers, but I had worked for well-connected people at the firm, and I had experience in one of the most sought-after areas on Wall Street: the sales and trading floor of a leading investment bank. Ricky didn't hesitate. He told me, "No. I'm not going to hire you."

I was crushed. I thought I'd done a good job. "I'll do whatever job you want," I pleaded. Then he told me something that I realize now was very wise. "It's not that you didn't do a good job," he said. "But you need to expand your horizons. You're too young to get wrapped up in this business. Go figure something else out. Try a different role. I don't want to see you get siloed into this business so early."

Looking back on it, Ricky's advice made sense—especially coming from him. Ricky was a financial and managerial genius, but he was also intellectually engaged with a wide world outside of finance. I remember he was always reading the newspaper and clipping articles to send to people. He'd sometimes send me out to buy books to send to his clients. He actually owned a couple of Jewish newspapers in Connecticut and was a leader in his community. He was a Wall Street professional, but he made sure to enrich his life—and other people's lives—by applying his intelligence to a wide range of interests. At the time, however, I was hurt and without a plan B.

I swallowed Ricky's rejection and pondered my options. What was I supposed to do? It was already April, and a lot of the best internship opportunities were taken, and besides, I couldn't afford to do unpaid work for the entire summer. Yale directed me to some internships specifically designed to get more Asian, African American, and Indian minorities onto Wall Street, but I didn't want any part of that. Then I remembered something Ricky suggested: that I look outside of the New York area and try out Washington, DC. "You've seen a little business. Why don't you see a little government?"

I decided to head to DC, with my Yale Alumni Directory in hand, and to sleep on a friend's couch until I found a job. I also decided to expand my network of advice and asked Marie Lugano, the coordinator of seminars and conferences at Bear Stearns, if she had any connections. Marie had been an unlikely friend at "the Bear" (as she called it) because of our different roles, but she was genuine and always supportive. I knew she was familiar with DC, and she had always been generous to me while I was working as a summer intern. I told her I was trying something new and was wondering if she knew of any paying jobs in politics for a student just out of their first year of college. Her answer surprised me. "Go see my friend Werner at the Willard Hotel. He runs the food and beverage operations. I'm sure he'll at least give you a job that pays."

The Willard Hotel? What was that? And what was I going to learn from a hotel job?

I soon discovered that the Willard, more formally known as the Willard Intercontinental, was a luxury hotel located on 1401 Pennsylvania Avenue, about two short blocks east of the White House and smack-dab in the heart of the American political bureaucracy. CEOs, lobbyists, journalists, entertainers, visiting politicians, ambassadors, and heads of state frequently stayed at the Willard. It was also a favorite gathering place of Washington's political class, a role it had served since the hotel was established in 1847. In fact, not long after it was founded, Nathaniel Hawthorne wrote, "The Willard Hotel more justly could be called the center of Washington than either the Capitol or the White House or the State Department." It is no surprise, then, that it became a featured backdrop in some of the great dramas of American history. Abraham Lincoln, for instance, stayed at the Willard before his inauguration in 1860, when he was under threat of assassination. Mark Twain, Harry Houdini, and Martin Luther King Jr.—who wrote his "I Have a Dream" speech at the hotel—had all stayed at the Willard.

I learned all these details from a history of the hotel that I devoured shortly after the Willard hired me as a temporary summer worker, filling in for different hotel employees as they took their two-week vacations. My first job was as a bellman. At no other time in my life would I meet so varied a stream of famous and interesting people as I did working at the Willard as a humble bellman. What was more, the work of a bellman was measured in tips. And I soon realized that the best way to get good tips was to treat guests like they were the most important people in the world, and one way to make the visiting CEOs or foreign dignitaries feel special was to tell them about how extraordinary the Willard was.

Say an important executive showed up with his entourage. As I walked through the lobby with their bags, I would say, "Let me tell you a little bit about the Willard. Do you see this hallway? That's known as Peacock Alley, a favorite spot for Washington power brokers in the nineteenth century. And see that chair? President Ulysses S. Grant used to sit in a chair in the same place"—and I'd show them the famous spot—"and enjoy a cocktail and cigar at the end of the day."

At this point, I had their attention.

"But people soon figured out that this is where the president was hanging out," I continued, "so representatives of various interest groups would huddle in the lobby nearby, waiting for their moment to intrude on Grant's moment of relaxation. Their presence so enraged the president that he was reported to have shouted, 'Damn lobbyists!'" At that moment, I would shake my fist for emphasis. "Though it was uttered over a hundred years ago, the term is still used today."

Sharing tidbits of history like this amused the guests—many of them members of the profession Grant despised—and their pleasure turned into my profit. I soon noticed I was receiving more and bigger tips, so I challenged myself to land at least one $50 tip—highly appropriate, given that President Grant was on the $50 bill. While I never did get a Grant-size thank-you, I was pleased to collect many $20 tips and came to appreciate seeing President Andrew Jackson's face on those bills.

After my stint as a bellman was over, I moved to the front desk. A few weeks later, I was a valet, driving fancy cars with the brand-new driver's license I'd recently gotten. After this, I was assigned to security, where I worked under a man who used to be the head of the Capitol Hill Police. On my first day, he showed me the rounds and then sent me on my way with nothing more than some keys, a flashlight, and a walkie-talkie. "If you see anything, give me a call."

While I was doing my rounds, I found myself near the roof. *I guess I should check it out,* I thought to myself. I had keys to the door and was a fully deputized member of the security team, after all. Literally thirty seconds after I'd walked outside, my boss burst onto the roof and tackled me.

"You can't be here!" he shouted.

"What are you talking about?" I replied. "You said I should look around!"

As he hurried to the door, he explained: "We are in sniper range of the White House—you'd have been shot in the next thirty seconds!"

Another lesson learned.

CHAPTER 10

WATCH ACTIONS, NOT WORDS

The Willard was helping me replenish my bank account while affording me life lessons, but it left me wanting something more. And so I started my search for an internship that would complement my new interest in politics by turning to the first page of the alumni directory. In those pre-internet days, it was a bound book filled with the names, jobs, and contact information of Yale's large network of former students. Near the top, I saw the American Enterprise Institute (AEI), a public policy think tank, and thought I'd give it a shot. Aside from hearing about it as a destination for former Bush administration officials, I knew little about AEI.

One of AEI's senior scholars caught my eye: James R. Lilley, class of '55, who had recently finished a stint as US ambassador to China under the George H. W. Bush administration. It was a part of the world I knew only a little about, which made me insatiably curious. Marty Miller had given me insight into the fall of the Soviet Union via my trip to Czechoslovakia. Bear Stearns had given me a front-row seat at the implosion of the so-called Japanese Economic Miracle. With the rest of the world, I'd watched, appalled, as Chinese troops gunned down Chinese citizens in Tiananmen Square because they were calling for democratic reforms. Of the three, the last was the hardest for me to wrap my head around. What might inspire a government to attack its own people? With a copy of my résumé in hand, I marched over to AEI on 17th Street—a fifteen-minute walk from the Willard—and secured an interview with Ambassador Lilley, which led to an internship for the summer with him and several other AEI scholars.

It was an encounter that shaped my academic future. Lilley was a fascinating guy. The son of an oil executive, he was born in Qingdao, China, in 1928, and there, he learned to speak fluent Mandarin and French as a young man. He did a brief stint in the US Army before attending Yale, George Washington University, Hong Kong University, and Columbia. In 1951, he joined the CIA, and after a few decades, he became its primary intelligence expert on China. He was a formal, rigid, and deeply caring man who understood, even then, the opportunities and challenges that China would present to the world as it increasingly engaged economically and politically with the United States.

Like most Americans, I didn't understand China. Working at AEI gave me an invaluable opportunity to dig deep, read widely, and address my curiosity. Working for Ambassador Lilley and Dr. Chong-Ping Lin, a Taiwanese scholar at AEI who also taught at Georgetown, I read everything I could find on subjects related to China, its military modernization, US-China trade policy, and human rights issues. And when time permitted, I helped other groups at AEI, including the Seminars & Conferences group, where I had the opportunity to work with David Gerson, one of the two main leaders of AEI, who has been a mentor since. Helping David as he organized events for the public gave me broad exposure to the work of a think tank while complementing the focused efforts I exerted with the Asian Studies group. And David taught me about the politics of personalities and how important it was to give thought to something as trivial as choosing who sits where during events with high-profile attendees.

Having just started studying political philosophy at Yale, I was fascinated by the Chinese Communist Party (CCP) and its unwavering focus on stability, no matter the costs. Those costs include the Chinese citizens killed in Tiananmen Square. They also included systemic censorship and domestic and international disinformation campaigns. Frankly, it reminded me of some warped mix of Huxley's *Brave New World* and Orwell's *1984*. And it underscored one of the most valuable lessons I learned from observing both Dr. Lin and Ambassador Lilley: They simply refused to believe anything the CCP said. They brought a skeptical eye to every development and felt deception was often behind official statements. In fact, I still recall Ambassador Lilley's warning: "Watch China's actions, not their words . . . deception is part of their way."

AEI was—and remains—a hotbed of political thought from the center-right, and I encountered many fellows that year who were already famous intellectual leaders in conservative circles or on the brink of national fame. It wasn't uncommon to see people like Dick Cheney, Robert Bork, Jeanne Kirkpatrick, or Charles Murray sitting in AEI's lunchroom or playing chess with interns. It was an exciting place for a college student interested in political ideas and how those ideas can bring about real change. Except for my work with Ambassador Lilley, I was on the periphery of all those other thinkers, but the fact that their ideas mattered outside of classrooms was palpable.

At the end of a day working at AEI, I would go to the Willard and start another shift. That became the rhythm of a strange summer, one during which I again shuttled between a working-class life and a life among elites. One moment, I would be carrying bags for guests at the hotel or walking security rounds, and the next, I'd be rubbing shoulders with intellectuals at one of the most prestigious think tanks in the country, working to translate ideas into influence and, ultimately, policy. I got to see different attitudes about the issues of the day. For instance, at AEI, I might be asked to research a public policy issue by analyzing comparative patent data in China and America to determine how property rights affect innovation capacity. Then, at the Willard, I'd strike up a conversation with the chief of security and end up learning that his unvarnished opinion on gun control was simple: "Enforce existing laws; don't limit my rights. Do you want to discuss speech control?"

As was true for all of my life, I understood there were insights to be learned as both an intern at AEI and a bellhop at the Willard. Despite its fancy clientele, the Willard was a good balance to the elite bubbles that I'd found myself in at Blair, Yale, Bear Stearns, and now AEI. Those institutions certainly opened my eyes to how power operated in the world. But I learned just as much getting dinner in Adams Morgan with an Ethiopian immigrant colleague who worked with me at the Willard. Hard work, it turned out, was a universal accelerant of one's learning, as was empathy and the ability to hear what people are saying, understand what they are thinking. The migrant mindset and a both-and mentality were proving powerful and useful tools with which to navigate life.

By the time August arrived, I saw that Ricky Greenfield had been right in not rehiring me for another summer at Bear Stearns. My exposure to the world of banking during high school had been invaluable, but until that summer, it had been my only professional experience. I had no idea that I could feel just as engaged and passionate about working at a think tank or take equal pride in working at the Willard. I also had a sense of having avoided a self-fulfilling rut. Toward the end of my first summer internship at AEI, I distinctly recall David asking me on the rooftop of the organization's 17th Street offices (which were safely out of sharpshooters' lines of sight) if I needed help lining up another internship. Recalling the lesson of my stock-certificate days in Brooklyn, I opted to set my goal as high as I could—any internship would be welcome, so why not see if the most interesting one was available? "How about the White House?" I asked. It was, after all, the pinnacle of world influence and political power. Heck, merely entering the building would be thrilling. David's response was straightforward: "Okay."

And to his credit, he delivered an introduction that led to a short stint at 1600 Pennsylvania Avenue, where I helped with correspondence for a week and then spent three weeks on the "Reinventing Government" work being led by then vice president Al Gore. All before returning to AEI to dig deeper into Chinese military modernization. And to round out the White House and AEI, I also worked at the Willard throughout the summer of 1994, filling in wherever and however needed.

In pushing me to try something other than just finance, Ricky's greatest gift was the opportunity to see that Bear Stearns, the employees and guests of the Willard, the White House staff, and the brains at AEI held no special insight into the one best path. Each contributed a bit to my own appreciation of the best way I could use my gifts. And that wouldn't have been possible if I'd siloed myself into any prescribed career at a young age, as so many students at elite institutions do to this day. Slowly but surely, I was becoming a generalist.

It wouldn't be until 2014 that William Deresiewicz, a Yale professor, put a name to this phenomenon: excellent sheep. But on my return to New Haven, I saw the evidence for it. All around me, I saw students who, having spent their lives worrying about good grades and checking off the right experiences, did so with the expectation of reaching the next rung up a common ladder. They didn't realize that there were other ladders, or that you didn't need to be on a ladder at all. And universities were complicit in funneling many of their brightest students into a few career paths. When I returned to Yale in the fall, invigorated by what I had learned and experienced, I finalized plans to double major in two multidisciplinary subjects—East Asian studies and Ethics, Politics & Economics. It was sufficiently off the presumptive path that Yale required me to seek a special petition.

CHAPTER 11

PRACTICAL WISDOM

For my junior summer, the one that leads to full-time employment for most students, I again opted to break convention. I decided to go to China and sought the necessary financial support to make the trip possible. I applied to and won numerous fellowships and was able to scrape together almost $3,000 in grants to fund the trip; I also obtained financial aid to attend the Princeton-in-Beijing immersive Mandarin program for the summer of 1995. And once I arrived in Beijing, I managed to secure an internship at the US embassy, working in the US Foreign and Commercial Service to help American businesses sell products and services to China.

Being on a shoestring budget, however, meant flying to Hong Kong and then out of Shanghai. *Great*, I thought, *an opportunity to travel!* And thanks to my trusty Lonely Planet guide, I was able to see more than twenty cities and towns across China. As a student tourist in the People's Republic, I was only partially lulled into the understanding that I was one more foreigner traversing another culture and country, as my father had done in Africa. Partially, but never completely, because I knew China was different.

One particular experience from my internship at the US embassy remains ingrained in my memory, and to this day, it influences how I think about China. It was the summer of 1995, and the embassy staff was frenetically arranging the details of three big China announcements: (1) Chrysler would be investing in the country to create a minivan factory, (2) China would be purchasing dozens of Boeing aircraft, and (3) American technology companies would be hired to install airport systems across the nation. In every meeting I attended, our Chinese counterparts would hammer out details and then confirm that there was "one China based in Beijing," an implicit statement about Taiwan.

Yet later that summer, Taiwan's president Lee Teng-hui arrived in Ithaca, New York, for his Cornell reunion. There, he was greeted not only by CNN cameras but also by numerous high-ranking elected American officials. Back in China, this created chaos. All three contract signings were canceled. Perhaps more telling, the Chinese moved forward with those contracts—but only after replacing the names of the companies. Europe's Airbus replaced America's Boeing; the German firm Daimler replaced Chrysler (this was years before the two merged); and the German firm Siemens, I recall, took the electronics work away from Hughes and other US companies.

The message delivered was clear: Taiwan is part of China; the government of the United States doesn't seem to understand that, so perhaps the American business community will help convey the message. This seemingly small event more than twenty-five years ago continues to haunt me because I sense many American companies have, in fact, become so focused on business opportunities that they've de facto been hijacked by the Chinese Communist Party and are made to (inadvertently) promote its causes.

As interesting as that summer abroad was, it didn't help me secure post-college employment. More important to me was that it gave me a deeper understanding of China and provided unique insights that made their way into both of my senior essays—one of which was about the role of deception in Chinese strategic thinking, whereas the other focused on the forthcoming expansionism of the Communist regime.

I have never regretted my decision not to follow the more conventional path, not to pursue a well-delineated academic route that would seamlessly lead to a career in law or finance after graduation. I saw too many of my classmates at Yale turn away from subjects they felt passionate about, lured not so much by the siren song of Wall Street as by the gravity of convention. They were living, I thought, by a script written by others, in its way no different from the script others had written when they'd come up with the Pre-Registration Orientation Program. There were prescribed ways for prescribed people to be, and if you'd only adhere to the script, you would, eventually, live long enough to no longer be aggrieved, maybe even happy.

I'd pushed against this from the outset of my Yale career. A tragedy shortly after graduation brought home in an indelible way how empty this promise could be. Big-hearted, hugely talented Nick Adamo succeeded in school, football, and life until his death in a plane crash less than a year after we'd been granted our degrees. Because of who Nick was and how he chose to live, I know that while the world was robbed of a talent, he was present and contributing to his fullest ability. And he hadn't done so by following anyone's prescribed choices.

After graduation, Nick had accepted a job as a salesman with Seerlip and Seerlip, an insurance firm in New Jersey. Being an insurance salesman was not exactly a typical post-college career choice among Ivy League graduates, but Nick had his clearly understood reasons. He did it to help his dad and be close to his girlfriend. He was on his way to a life of meaning, by being Nick. Along the way, he mingled his ambitions, personal and professional, with public servants he admired. In fact, he died in a private plane crash in a craft piloted by Elmer Schaal, a WWII US Navy veteran and former mayor of Bridgewater, New Jersey. Nick had embodied a both-and life. Yale grad and working class. Football player and academic superstar. Family oriented and professionally ambitious. Aspiring and public-minded. Not a year goes by when I don't think about Nick.

Living a both-and life isn't easy. When I visit or teach at college campuses today, I see all these brilliant minds preparing for a world with so many tough problems that need better solutions. How do we best provide economic development to poor countries? What are the best ways to secure the rule of law in unstable societies? How can we improve the way we curate art to enrich people's lives? How can we cure cancer? How do we ensure a stable world in which democracy and opportunity hold greater sway than top-down directives? Rather than casting wide nets for useful knowledge to help address these foundational questions, many of the talented students instead default to asking a much less consequential question: What are the least surprising choices I could make that promise me a comfortable life with a beachhead, maybe even a beachfront home, in one of the world's elite bubbles?

Throughout my Yale career, I encountered a personally more confounding situation. I had learned the virtues of being an explorer, the value of a migrant mindset that met opportunity with the courageous courtesy of host and guest. It had been the touchstone to both of my parents making a new, meaningful life in a new country. And it had provided me with a set of principles with which to navigate my early life, all the way to a Yale undergraduate degree. But the better I performed against the most popular metrics of elite American success, the more uncomfortable my parents became with any divergence from those metrics.

CHAPTER 12

JACKASS OF MANY PURSUITS

It was at Yale that I learned a phrase that traces back to at least the eighteenth century: "Even a broken clock is correct twice a day." To this was added the professor's quip: "Even a blind squirrel finds a nut every now and then." A student had guessed a right answer, and the professor cited the blind-squirrel anecdote to say that even the misguided and inefficient sometimes get lucky. Do your research, she was saying, and know your facts rather than guessing. Even as she said it, however, I took away a different lesson. I'd spent four years going from class to class, department to department, listening to highly trained academics expound on narrow subjects they knew thoroughly. After I heard my professor make that observation about blind squirrels, I had a different thought. What do you call a squirrel who never moves from atop its overstuffed bag of nuts? A specialist. Over time, it was becoming increasingly obvious that I just didn't fit the mold. I was intellectually restless and was realizing, with every passing pressure to specialize, that I was more fox than hedgehog. I was a generalist.

My post-college years are best understood as a series of successful, self-inflicted, and ultimately, immensely useful confusions. In following this pattern, I was squarely in the majority. The newly minted graduate who is 100 percent certain of what she is to spend her life doing, with whom, and where is a unicorn. Though such creatures might exist, I wasn't one of them, and neither was anyone else I knew. The problem was, we weren't allowed to admit it. The explicit spirit of exploration with which we'd begun our studies had been replaced by a pantomime of conviction. What do you think you'll major in?—the conversation starter of my freshman and sophomore years—had morphed into What will your profession be?

I was living the life of a wide-eyed squirrel who was occasionally mistaken for being blind, which struck me then, as it does now, as unfair. Awkwardly, the confusion began with my parents. They were immensely proud of the path I'd taken to Blair and Yale. So, too, were family and friends. But as graduation came closer and closer, the questions became more direct. During my early years at Yale, the questions were attached to what I was studying. Was it going to be physics? If not physics, then would my classwork direct me toward a premed degree? Or perhaps my interest in political philosophy hinted at forthcoming applications to law schools? And why these courses in Chinese culture? Eventually, the questions weren't about *what* I was studying and instead, more bluntly, *why* are you studying *that*?

"Vikram," my parents would ask, "what will you ever do with *that*?"

They had always encouraged my sister and me to explore life, pursue interests, and most importantly, gain knowledge, and they continued to do so. But with each passing semester I was at Yale, they introduced a new notion: "What will all this effort and knowledge amount to?" And eventually, "What job are you going to have—how will you be employed?" To their credit, my parents didn't sugarcoat their concerns in that much vaguer question, "Vikram, what are you going to do with your life?" They were far more direct: "Vikram, how will you make a living?"

As a doctor? No. Then perhaps as a lawyer? No. Well, maybe an engineer? No, not that. So, as an accountant or banker? To which I usually offered up a *maybe*. Which satisfied no one.

For many of my parents' acquaintances, a banker stood behind a counter, perhaps sat at a desk, and helped customers open accounts or secure a loan. Serious people, yes, but somehow not what they thought I would do with my degree from Yale.

Often, I couldn't escape the impression that my parents had shifted their perspectives. It had been their generation's responsibility to explore, wander, and bear risks amid uncertainty so that their children wouldn't have to. Not wanting my sister or me to struggle as much as they had, that I understood. What parent doesn't want better for their kids? But all the value, work ethic, and possibilities inherent in exploring, wandering, and bearing risks—what they had both done in pursuit of opportunities—were seductively appealing. These were virtues to be pursued, perhaps improved upon. In principle, my parents agreed. In practice, they hoped to see me quickly, successfully, settled with a steady income and responsible respectability. And that meant to be a doctor or a lawyer or an engineer or—expressed with a sigh of regret—maybe even a banker.

I had spent four years resisting Yale's best efforts to put me in a silo—first as a minority, then as one sort of major rather than another, and finally as a clearly declared profession-bound undergraduate. All around me, I saw the best and brightest head off with mostly feigned confidence into careers, round pegs into round holes, square ones aligned with square holes. In private, many of my friends admitted to uncertainty. Publicly, however, they declared themselves. Most went into some branch of finance, and whether this was due to an inherent interest in how Wall Street fueled the capitalist engine that powered our lives or because it offered a shorter path to wealth, I cannot say. A large minority immediately began preparing for the next required degree. A few intended to have careers in government. Fewer still wanted to be professional scholars.

My difficulties arose not because I disliked the well-marked paths but rather from the fact that I liked aspects of many of them. Expressing this, though, seemed like a dead end. Previously, I had encountered smorgasbords. Blair, Bear Stearns, Yale, the Willard, the American Enterprise Institute—each was an explicit invitation to try this, do that, learn a bit from each, and apply what I learned to whatever I turned to next. Now, however, I saw forks in the road. I was too old, or so it was implied, to dabble. As one recent alum colorfully advised, "You don't want to be a jackass of many pursuits, master of none."

No, no, I did not. But wasn't there a path toward being a master of many pursuits and no one's specific jackass? How had breadth gone from a desired perspective to a liability? Surely, breadth and depth both had roles in society? Surely breadth was not bad, was it? I'd never been good at just going along with what others were doing. Even as a kid, I knew that there was a handful of formulaic solutions for many problems . . . but I was always curious. Weren't there other options?

At each juncture of my young adult life, uncertainty ruled the day. The facts before me might be all the facts there were, but maybe not. Framed that way, each instance became an exploration. Instead of presumptive full stops, I learned to ask more questions. There were private schools, for example. Well, how did those work? I would need a scholarship. Okay, apply for one. The one offered was insufficient. Well, who might help make up the difference? Could he also help with an internship? Moving stock certificates in a Brooklyn warehouse could be the entirety of a Bear Stearns internship. Or maybe not. It is only a little too glib to say these were all replays of the hands-free shower. After all, the touchstone of that idea had been that washcloth and soap might be the best of all possible ways to wash, but maybe not. Put simply, from an early age, I'd been introduced to the idea that what was better wasn't certain. And if that was the case, why not figure out if better is an option?

Rather than a problem, uncertainty became a strategy, though for most of my childhood, that is too grandiose a term for it. During my first eighteen years, "Why not?" often led to "What the hell!" which ended in "How best to go about it?" Which, as a lived habit, worked less and less well over the four years I studied at Yale. Each year I was in New Haven, I experienced the wash-and-rinse cycle of an institution built to winnow away uncertainty. Again and again,

I sat in classrooms at the front of which stood renowned experts, women and men acclaimed for their in-depth mastery of a subject. Whether interpreting a poem or explaining the laws of physics, professors addressed students gathered to scribble down received wisdom. It wasn't that the professors closed off debate—not at all—it was that everyone understood that the debates ended after the expert in the room, having dutifully listened to the class, spoke up. It's only in retrospect, with more than a quarter century of hindsight, that I can see how such a system might produce a dystopia more representative of Huxley's *Brave New World* than that of Orwell's *1984*. Unlike Orwell's world, in which independent thinking was actively stamped out, Huxley's world was marked by a conditioning that undermined it. Censoring was replaced by self-censoring. And sometimes, something more insidious—a self-censoring that could mute inquisitive doubt, curiosity, and quite possibly, solutions to the most intractable of problems.

The longer I was at Yale, the more it made me feel antsy. I always wanted to understand what the reasoning was behind an expert's opinion, the "first principles" of what was going on. Immediately after glimpsing such principles, I wondered whether that solution would work for me. Might another solution, perhaps one not yet even considered, work better? That was the appeal of political philosophy. A hidden insight learned from studying political thought is that one person's ideal way forward was often another person's worst outcome, and both could be utterly reasonable positions.

In some instances, common sense wasn't common, and to a few individuals, it didn't even make sense. Disentangling that knot was when things got interesting or, as political history taught, tragic. When the possibility of tragic outcomes grew, wasn't uncertainty preferable to certainty? Wasn't the search for the unthought, untried solution better than accepting no solution at all? Why settle for bad outcomes as foregone conclusions?

My instinct to question received wisdom was paired with a related tendency to buck expectations that others placed on me. The migrant mindset is the mindset of fiercely independent thinking, one of "I will forge my own path." As I had learned at both the Willard and AEI, this reflected an old instinct common to strangers in a promising new land. It was also the gift of anyone willing to question conventional thinking. Another insight born of studying political philosophy was the appreciation—one that grew with time—that most of America's Founding Fathers were exemplars of the migrant mindset. Warts and all, they questioned their world's status quo, and warts and all, they embraced uncertainty in the belief that better was attainable. And for generation after generation, Americans have kept faith with that belief, navigating toward an ever more perfect union, a process that attracted the commitment and dedication of millions, my parents among them.

CHAPTER 13

"To Pay What Is Owed"

At twenty-two with a newly printed college degree, I wasn't that ambitious or cocksure. I wanted to do something interesting. I had friends heading off to careers wearing new suits and confident faces. I had family whispering and even outright asking, "What, Vikram, has been the point of it all?"

It's not like I had been completely impractical in my education, of course—I had, after all, worked hard to get excellent grades at a top university. But now that I was faced with seemingly limitless options, I was not sure which way to go. There were so many possibilities. Analysis paralysis set in. I would have liked to go into the US Foreign Service right away—to pursue a diplomatic career or work in some globally oriented job. I even met with officers in the Armed Services Recruiting Office in New Haven because serving my nation intrigued me. One possibility I didn't have, however, was sitting on the sidelines. To graduate from Yale, I had incurred debt, and there was nothing to fall back on other than the next paycheck.

Life's sticks and carrots were plainly visible. While the wealthy at Yale came out with an Ivy League degree, I had come out with a degree and a small mountain of debt. One problem was abundantly clear—whatever I was going to do, I would have to make money doing it so that I could pay back my loans and be able to help my parents and family.

For me, this was more than a mere intention; it was a moral obligation. Well before I attended Yale, I would have awkwardly expressed the same idea, though drawing on notions of trust and courtesy, of the common decencies that anchor good guests and good hosts. Yale, and the political theory classes I threw myself into, crystallized this as a moral obligation. Because of my degree, I could hold court with the best of them at a colloquium on political history. Gathered in a classroom, we budding academics would cite sources to explain, "Before it was codified in law, moral obligation was backstopped by an honor-bound duty to fulfill an obligation, a debt." And someone else would add, "Laws and rules governing professions would arise to turn moral obligation into a foundational principle that enables property rights and most commercial exchanges." A third would chime in as the professor nodded agreement: "But it remains a community-grounded expectation that we each act honorably."

Years earlier, however, I had learned this as a simple tenet of conduct: "We meet our obligations." Toward the end of my high school years, as I mentioned earlier, we lost our family home along with my father's gas station. That his station was struggling was understood by all of us, in the ways that all families understand financial stresses. I recall seeing it in the extra hours he worked, in the shift to less expensive groceries, in the concern on my parents' faces. Eventually, over breakfast, it was made clear to my sister and me that the gas station *and* our home were going so that my father could meet his obligations, even under bankruptcy.

"Why must we move?" I recall my sister asking.

My father was factual. "To pay what is owed, my love."

"That means our house?"

"Yes. The gas station, the house."

My mom didn't miss a beat. "We will be fine. A change, yes, but that's not new. We will be fine, I promise."

Later, I came to appreciate that my father had been poorly advised when he bought the gas station. He could have done so under a limited liability corporation structure, which, if the worst happened, would have protected our personal assets, our home. The worst turned out to be that the large factory across the street from his gas station reduced its number of shifts during an economic slowdown, reducing a stream of daily cars and customers to a trickle. Nothing he did caused it, and nothing he could have done would have prevented it. And when the worst did happen, his business obligations flowed to our family.

We recovered, but the damage my father's credit endured from the bankruptcy was brutal. I remember making sense of things by connecting the experience with something I'd learned in my high school Latin class. The concept of "credit" stemmed from *credite*, meaning "to trust." Losing the world's trust at the beginning of one's career was something I did not want to have happen. Meeting my student loans was a moral obligation, a matter of honor, an expectation of an individual in good standing as host and guest in a wider world. Even if it meant pursuing jobs that were not ideal for me or working longer hours than I would prefer, I never once questioned the need to repay the money I had borrowed.

I found a job as an energy analyst with the consulting firm Booz Allen & Hamilton, in the company's Houston office. It paid well, and a job in Texas meant no state or local income taxes. Additionally, the work would require travel, allowing me to visit friends and family with some regularity. In accepting the position, I figured, *Why not pay the least taxes while living in hotels?*

More challenging was that the first weeks felt like once again being tossed into the deep end. I, a twenty-two-year-old with little business experience and virtual ignorance of "business process reengineering," was expected to help companies like Exxon and Mobil (at the time, they were separate companies) become more efficient? My solution was to embrace my value as a fresh pair of eyes. I listened, read, watched, asked questions, and listened some more. The fresh perspective I offered did lead to questioning basic assumptions, but the usefulness of that tactic depended on the associate to whom I reported conveying my perspective upward through the filters between me and a client awaiting our analysis.

What I could control, I did, such as paying down my debts. I also took advantage of being far from Landing, New Jersey, or New Haven, Connecticut. I took two-step classes, frequented barbecue restaurants, and came to crave huevos rancheros for breakfast.

Universally welcoming, Texans also rarely missed the opportunity to remind me I was not a native Texan. This just meant the logic of guest and host was explicit. No surprise, but I took to it easily. If my Yale classmates who had jumped immediately to New York or Boston finance jobs regaled me with stories of filet mignon served during boardroom lunches, I answered with equal enthusiasm with stories of my dining at Dairy Queen alongside welders and oil-rig roughnecks. Sure, working at Booz Allen included the occasional fancier meal and nice hotel, but just about everyone I worked with in Houston moved easily from these to burgers, fries, and iced tea (unsweetened). Belonging boiled down to common acceptance that I was both a Yale graduate from New Jersey and also one cog in the vast enterprise of Texas energy production.

Well within eight months of arriving in Texas, I began to feel as if I had gotten my feet beneath me. Then, a relatively new Houston-based energy firm began aggressively recruiting everyone in Booz Allen's Houston office. I was also offered a job. But this opportunity looked less like the deep end and more like a whirlpool. I was simply and truly unable to understand what I would be doing. And no one I talked to, including representatives of the new firm, could explain it in a way that made sense to me. What didn't bother others, or at least not so much that they turned down handsome compensation packages, bothered me. I turned them down.

The name of the firm was Enron. Founded by industry veteran Kenneth Lay in 1985, Enron promised a unique means for risk management in the uncertain world of energy production. From oil and petrochemicals to "weather risk management," Enron claimed it could introduce certainty in famously volatile markets. Everything I knew—from life, my studies, and my time at Booz Allen—told me that the degree of certainty being promised was somewhere between very unlikely and completely impossible.

Fortunately, when the job couldn't pass my own sniff test—a plausible answer to "What would I be doing?"—I avoided becoming ensnared in the scandals that brought Enron to an end and racked up billions in shareholder losses. It turned out that not only was Enron unable to manage the uncertainty it claimed to manage, but it created uncertainty where there wasn't any, just to produce profits.

That I had dodged a bullet wasn't completely obvious for several years. Having said no to Enron more or less brought my stint in Texas to a close. Instead of sticking around the Lone Star State, I headed back to the Northeast and New York City. I had secured the most unquestioned response a recent Yale undergraduate can give friends and family about post-college life. I accepted a job in the Mergers and Acquisitions (M&A) Department at Merrill Lynch. I would be an investment banker.

M&A is a great starter job for a person who wants to understand the world of business in all its fascinating varieties. As an analyst for Merrill Lynch, I had to study and value companies in a wide range of industries—from the budding field of e-commerce to oil and gas pipelines—and dig deep into the details of how each individual business worked. Each company, each industry, was its own case study of shifting competitions within uncertainties. This not only taught me how different companies operated, but it also taught me *why* certain companies were more successful than others, and it forced me to think about how they could work better.

Of course, what I was tasked with doing was to jump into one end of the pool of possibilities so that I could climb out the other end with a conclusive recommendation. When you're in investment or corporate banking, it is usually very easy to measure success and failure. The only thing that matters is if something works, and working is visible in a company's fundamentals or their share price, if they're publicly traded. Sometimes you had to dig to discover them, but the shared understanding was that useful possibilities were there to be discovered. This forced me to have a very pragmatic approach to problem-solving, which Merrill Lynch taught me was invaluable.

Another reason I headed to the Big Apple was that it would put me closer to friends from Yale and Blair and, in particular, one beautiful young woman whom I simply couldn't stop thinking about: Kristen.

She was one year my junior and, in one of those great acts of dumb luck, the roommate of a freshman to whom I was assigned as an adviser. At Yale, Kristen and I spent years in the (mostly) joyous uncertainty of "sort of dating." We took ballroom dancing; attended formals; and shared stories during our Washington, DC, internships. In the process, we routinely confused our friends as to whether or when we were boyfriend and girlfriend. It was only after I went to study abroad in China and we started sending postcards to each other that I finally realized that my feelings for her, and I hoped hers for me, went beyond an on-again, off-again dating friendship.

By the time my Booz Allen position dried up, Kristen had graduated from Yale and was working at a public finance advisory firm in Philadelphia. We had stayed in touch while I was in Texas, even traded visits, and as I considered my options, I knew there was an unwavering desire to explore more fully what we meant to each other.

No doubt, New York City is closer to Philadelphia than Houston. But Merrill Lynch was an all-in job. My weekend trips south to Philly became frequent, but I juggled our relationship around "bankers' hours." It was what my mother called them, and they were, for her, a source of endless confusion.

During my first year at Merrill Lynch, Mother's Day fell on a Sunday, and I told my mom I would call her from work. Her reply was, "But doesn't the bank close on Sundays?" The M&A

Department never closed, and my work life felt fragile, precarious, subject to the whims of an associate or vice president. And my relationship with Kristen felt the uncertainty of scheduling. Yes, we managed hasty dinners galore. But almost all of them ended with my returning to the office after a 9:00 p.m. meal.

It wasn't easy to make time for each other during that first year I was in New York—we were both working demanding jobs that expected us to be in the office ninety hours a week. But when I could, I'd take the train to Philadelphia and explore the city and its many great restaurants with Kristen, or she'd come to New York and do the same. Sometimes what we could manage to do together was memorable for all the wrong reasons. I was once so busy that our date consisted of takeout Chinese food eaten in the Merrill Lynch lobby because I needed to get back to my desk, where I would work until midnight. Hours like that were not uncommon. Still, we found a way to keep our relationship going.

After two years of this busy back-and-forth life, Kristen got accepted into Harvard Law School, and my two-year analyst program came to an end. I had survived the weird hazing rituals of the M&A banking world, the long hours, and the competitive focus of sustained attention. It was a rite of passage. But having passed, I didn't want to stay. It was time to make another important life choice. Stay in New York City, close to Wall Street, or not?

In the end, it wasn't tough. It was clear to me I couldn't both be an investment banker and have a life with Kristen. I decided to follow her, taking a job at Great Hill Partners, a private equity firm with offices in downtown Boston.

CHAPTER 14

A Pigeon, Castle, and Proposal

Our first few years in Boston were fun for a simple reason: they were the best either-or years of our lives. Either we were at work—for me, the firm; for Kristen, Harvard Law School—or we were enjoying ourselves. In one domain of life, we telegraphed certainty: Yale- and Harvard-trained finance and legal professionals pursuing significant careers at serious places. In the other, we telegraphed confident curiosity: amateur golfers and adventurous international travelers. Though we worked hard, we had more time and money, and what's more, we were finally together and growing even closer as a couple. Hard work and frugality meant that my college loans were paid off, and we could afford to travel with the extra money I was bringing in. We were enjoying all that Boston had to offer, too. We also knew, with slowly growing clarity, that it couldn't last.

Some of our friends were starting to get engaged. Kristen and I had been a couple for years. It was impossible not to have the thought of marriage enter our minds. I admit, however, it was a prospect I viewed with trepidation. That we loved and cared for each other was obvious. That we enjoyed each other's company was long established. We were also independent. Absolutely, we had common interests and common ambitions. But we also pursued and were protective of our individual interests and ambitions.

As time marched forward, dominoes began to fall. Kristen's closest friend, Maria, got engaged. Then my closest friend, Eric, got engaged. As we attended friends' weddings, the questions, implied and direct, about what our future as a couple was going to be were asked. Then Kristen made a very concrete, rational decision. She had been living at Harvard Law School and would graduate in 2002. I lived on Beacon Hill, a Boston neighborhood sandwiched between the downtown business district and the Charles River. She had interned with a Boston firm in 2000. She was planning on taking the Massachusetts Bar Exam, a choice I knew she was making at least partially based on me. We would stay together, live in the small Beacon Hill apartment, walk to our offices. Rationally, it all made sense. I was irrationally thrilled.

What I knew to a certainty by then was that when I enjoyed moments of excitement, like getting appointed to my first board, I wanted to celebrate with Kristen. Indeed, I couldn't imagine celebrating with anyone but her. Similarly, when I was confused and needed a thinking partner, I turned to her. And when down or depressed, I sought her.

The first rule of a life lived in uncertainty is to allow uncertainty to be fun.

In November of 2000, Kristen was in her second year of law school. This is when most law school students start interviewing at law firms, hoping to land a position ahead of graduation a year away. Because it would be too difficult for students to schedule their interviews around the law school's rigorous academic schedule, Harvard, like many law schools, had what was called a "fly-out week," when classes were canceled so that students could travel to the various law firms and businesses around the country that were interested in employing them. No surprise, Kristen had so distinguished herself that she didn't need to travel. She had already worked summer jobs at a small boutique intellectual property law firm in New York and in the Boston office of the highly prestigious firm Ropes & Gray. Both had offered her a full-time job, and she had already committed to staying in Boston. A consequence of her already having a job lined up meant she had a rare week off. This was a fantastic opportunity, and I didn't want to let it go to waste. "Great," I said, "can I plan a vacation?" She agreed, and I suggested we do a golf trip—we were both starting to get into golf, and this would be a chance to fly to a cool course somewhere and relax and play a few rounds. Or at least that's what I wanted her to believe.

I left some brochures about various golf courses in North Carolina and hinted that that was where we were going. Meanwhile, I grabbed her passport and tucked it away with mine. We took our first flight from Logan to Newark, where I told Kristen we would catch a connecting flight. When we landed in New Jersey, I informed Kristen that our flight was boarding and that we were farther from the gate than anticipated. "Come with me, quickly!" I said and hustled her through the airport to our departure gate, where a flight was leaving for Dublin, Ireland.

The destination wasn't the only surprise. I'd collected all the airline miles and credit card points I'd accumulated in my life to get us first-class seats for the leg to Dublin. It was really exciting, and Kristen was clearly having a good time. She also noticed the bag I was clutching the entire trip. I wouldn't let the cab driver or the bellman at the hotel in Ireland touch it. No one was taking that bag.

In Dublin, we toured the Guinness brewery and enjoyed a solid forty-five-minute conversation with a Welshman whose accent was so strong we only understood every fifth word. Best we could tell, he had a pet pigeon that had somehow crossed the Atlantic Ocean, and British Airways and Aer Lingus had flown the bird back to him, first class. The story was hilarious, at least to us, and in retrospect, that may have had more to do with our beverage consumption than just a wacky fella from Wales. To this day, when thinking of travel, Kristen and I can't help but imagine a transatlantic flight with a wayward Welsh pigeon in first class. We enjoyed pub food that evening as we walked back to the hotel.

And the next day, I told her it was time to take our clubs to the other side of the island, where we could golf. We rented a car and drove through the beautiful Irish countryside, often getting lost along the way. (This was, of course, before smartphones.) We'd occasionally stop and ask for directions, and inevitably, the response we received was "Straight on." At first, this gave us confidence, until one young lady shared that advice as we headed into a roundabout. We couldn't stop laughing. The trip was among the most comical of our lives—think National Lampoon's Irish vacation. It was slapstick, but it was real. Our journey to the golf course took three hours longer than expected, and we barely arrived in time for our afternoon tee time. When we pulled through the stone gates at Ashford Castle (where the sign reads EXCELLENCE SINCE 1228), we were met with a stunning sight. And for those who are unfamiliar with Ashford Castle, picture a storybook castle with rolling hills in the foreground and a lake beyond, a stone bridge over a meandering brook that looks, for all intents and purposes, like a moat. It had to be among the most romantic sites either of us had ever seen.

After we settled in, we changed and headed out for nine holes of golf. With birds of prey overhead, deer on the fairway, and mist emanating from the lake over the castle, it was truly magical. Kristen, unable to contain herself in the setting, cutely asked, "Is today a special day?" I chuckled and played on, feigning a seriousness to my golf to conceal my own nervousness.

We unpacked after golf, and I told her I'd made reservations at the restaurant. We got ready for dinner. While she got dressed, I went out to get flowers. And then, before we walked to the castle's dining room, I gave her the flowers and then finally revealed what I'd been carrying in the precious bag: "I wanted to give you something," I said, and took out a small box, which she excitedly opened. In it, she found a necklace. The necklace had a heart with a sapphire on one side and an emerald on the other. "The sapphire is for your blue eyes, and the emerald is for Ireland—to remind you of this trip." Kristen was the embodiment of both-and, both pleased and perplexed, both grateful and disappointed. We went to dinner with an awkwardness that is hard to describe. We dined and made conversation about the golf and the beauty of the setting. Eventually, Kristen could no longer bite her tongue. Over entrées, she blurted out, "You know, if you were going to propose, this was the time and place to do it! I mean, it's fine you didn't, but it's just too perfect. Why would you not? I just don't understand what's going on here!"

One of the things I love about Kristen is that when she's got something on her mind, she has a hard time keeping it to herself. She wasn't angry so much as bewildered. Who goes to such lengths and doesn't propose?

Despite some fits and starts to the conversation, we managed to have a nice, even wonderful, dinner. We'd been together for years, and Kristen stepped easily into both enjoying herself and calling out my romantic missteps. Afterward, I gamely asked her if she wanted to take a walk along the lake that was next to the hotel. It was just us and the lake and the castle, and a clear sky with stars reflecting on the water. And that's where I actually proposed. Yes, I'd brought the ring with me. In fact, I'd asked her father for permission before we left America.

Kristen said yes. She also told me she loved the proposal, though she forever held to the belief that I played out the bait-and-switch game for hours longer than needed. Maybe. But I wanted her to feel surprised. I had boarded that plane with the ring in my possession and her parents' approval. At no point was I uncertain of what was going to happen. The only uncertainty was what her answer would be. Part of the fun of drawing out the moment was the authenticity of her response, once given.

And thereafter, the rest of our weeklong trip was a marvelous series of golf games, castles, and joyful chats about our future before we had to return to our lives in Boston. The year we were engaged was a whirlwind of planning and work, all while Kristen finished her last year at Harvard Law School and I continued to work in Boston's financial district. All through the spring and summer of 2001, we were kept busy with the logistical slog of pending matrimony. Where were we going to get married? Who should cater? Live band or DJ? Who were we going to invite? On the last question, in my case, it was going to be a *lot* of people. Indian families tend to have big weddings. We arranged a trip to India in November so that we could hold many of the traditional events with my mother's and father's extended families, all before our official wedding, which would take place in December. For the latter, we were lucky to find an amazing old mansion in Newport, Rhode Island, that could handle the two hundred or so guests who had been invited.

As the summer went on, we selected caterers and food and wine and began to finalize the preparations for events in India and in the United States, all while continuing to work—me at my job and Kristen in her last year of law school. It was only a matter of time, however, before we were introduced to another rule of a life lived amid uncertainty: sometimes, despite an individual's best-laid plans and intentions, uncertainty will drop the floor out from under you, especially when it is unforeseeable.

CHAPTER 15

"ONE OF OURS?"

On a beautiful fall morning in 2001, everything was put into a new perspective. I was working in my office in downtown Boston when suddenly, computer screens and televisions were capturing the unfolding horror of downtown Manhattan. It was 9/11. Shortly after the second tower fell, all of us in the office were asked by security to immediately exit the building and go home.

It's difficult to capture how chaotic and uncertain everything was on that day, even in a city that was not under attack. As events unfolded—the two planes striking the World Trade Center (WTC), the plane that struck the Pentagon, the plane that heroic passengers forced to crash in a field in Pennsylvania—no one knew the extent of the attacks or when they would end. Facts were few and vague. It was rumored, and then revealed, that the two planes used to attack the WTC had departed from Boston. No one knew if more attacks were imminent. No one knew if Boston itself would be a target. The country—and with it, the world—was plunged into acute, commonly shared uncertainty.

Although Kristen lived in the Harvard Law School dormitories, she spent a lot of time over at my small Beacon Hill apartment. We both had cell phones, which were still relatively new in 2001. Texting wasn't common, so we spent hours trying to call one another, as did everyone else. The cell networks were overloaded, and neither of us could get through to the other. Given all that wasn't known, my best option was to walk to my apartment and assume she'd meet me there.

On that walk, I passed a convenience store in my neighborhood run by a Middle Eastern man. Beacon Hill is a very upscale neighborhood. It was just yards from everything and boasted the cobbled-street charms of Revolutionary-era Boston. This man had run a store there for many years, and he was a linchpin of the community—I used to stop by to purchase the odd soda, sandwich, or household item from him all the time. As I walked by his store, I heard the roaring noise of a fighter jet, flying low, over my head. I looked up, catching just a glimpse of a military plane I associated with the evening news, special sporting events, or a Fourth of July celebration.

The store owner had run out at the noise, anxiously glancing up. And then he asked me, "Do you think that's one of ours?"

I was momentarily stunned. My first thought being, *If the attackers actually have fighter jets, then this problem is much bigger than it already appears to be.* But having briefly seen the wing of the plane, I was able to assure him that it had been a US military jet. He nodded, whispered a "Thank God," and returned to his store.

Later, as I reflected on the store owner's words, I took comfort in the man's reaction. In his use of the words *one of ours* was a glimpse of the country's shared response to what had happened. He was of Arab descent, quite likely a Muslim, but he was also 100 percent American, and he was as worried as the rest of us. Like me, he was part of the great melting pot that allowed people from around the world to come to this great nation of ours with a common belief in the potential of every person.

Eventually, Kristen had taken the "T" (as the mass transit subway is called in the Boston area) from Harvard Square to the Massachusetts General Hospital stop, which was a mere four blocks from my apartment. We were glued to the television for the remainder of the day, in turns stupefied, horrified, and infuriated by what we were watching. We called family and friends, though most calls didn't get through. Merrill Lynch's offices were in the WTC complex, and among the uncertainties was whether friends and colleagues were alive or not. I was also receiving frantic calls from the wife of my best friend, Eric. He had been booked to fly from Boston to Los Angeles that morning on American Airlines. That airline's nonstop flight from Boston to LA was one of the two planes that had crashed into the WTC. For hours, we didn't know of Eric's whereabouts, whether he was alive or among the dead. Eventually, we heard from him. He had opted for a connecting flight, which was cheaper. He had been on a plane to Dallas, where he would have taken another plane to Los Angeles, but he was grounded in Texas. More important, he was alive. The same wasn't true of several friends from my time at Merrill Lynch who were working in the WTC towers.

After overwhelming confusion and slowly receding uncertainty, after learning of lives lost and many disrupted, we listened to President Bush give his speech from the remains of the WTC in Lower Manhattan. We quickly realized the world had changed. Against that backdrop of dust, ruin, and destruction, President Bush promised help for the afflicted and justice for the terrorists. The consequences, beginning with the global economy and international relations, would be profound.

While the world confronted a new reality, Kristen and I confronted a comparatively small—but for us, important—problem. We had to replan our wedding. We had to figure out how the new reality was going to affect the many plans we had made for that fall. One thing was certain: the India portion of the wedding was off. We also knew that many guests would not be flying to Rhode Island to attend a wedding anytime soon. In rapid order, we were forced to cancel arrangements we had made with our photographer, our florist, the caterer, and the restaurant where we planned to have our rehearsal dinner.

Nevertheless, we were able to pull together a ceremony in Newport in the short time before the appointed date, and it turned out beautifully. Confronted with the unforeseeable and the tragic, we concerned ourselves with the small portion of the world that was in our control, made adjustments, and kept going. We figured it out. Just like everyone else. And we were now husband and wife.

As we settled into our married lives, I started to take stock of my career. I had not planned on a life in finance, what my parents still called "being a banker," but there I was, working in private equity at Great Hill Partners. I had also been appointed to the boards of two portfolio companies. On paper, I had a very promising professional outlook for a young analyst, but something didn't feel right to me. I was successful, but professionally, I wasn't happy. By all outward appearances, I had been ticking off the right boxes, attaining the right degrees, taking the right steps when it came to adulthood, investments, and job switches. But I was unfulfilled.

It would take me a while to realize this, but I was coming to the end of my comfortable either-or existence. Being many different things in many different circumstances had worked great for years. I was either at home or at the office. I was either traveling for work or on vacation with Kristen. I was either a neighbor in Beacon Hill or an analyst working in Boston's financial district. I was either visiting family in New Jersey or attending a reunion of Blair or Yale alumni. I was confident in many different silos, but I struggled to connect a few, let alone all, of them. A big part of the problem was that I knew what was wrong—the dots weren't getting connected—but I didn't know how to solve it. For me, this suggested I didn't know enough, and that was a problem I knew how to solve.

The obvious choice after working a few years in banking was for me to get an MBA. But I wanted to enroll in a PhD program so that I could learn to *generate* knowledge. But what sort of knowledge? When you pursue a PhD, everyone expects you to narrow your focus and dive deep. Among experts, the PhD is the pinnacle of a discipline's pyramid. Except, I knew I wanted to *think differently*, to challenge myself and the way I had already been trained to look at the world. I wanted a degree that would widen my vision, not narrow it.

Nearly every American graduate program I investigated promised to do the opposite. From politics to math, scholarly departments training PhD candidates were devoted to a rigorous and narrow seven-year path of training that, at the end, would produce a unicorn who would be competitive in the job market seeking unicorns. It sounded dreadful.

Then one day in the early winter of 2001, as I walked out of our apartment on Beacon Hill, I looked to my right, and through the leafless trees, across the Charles River, I saw another option: the Massachusetts Institute of Technology (MIT).

That's kind of an interesting place, I thought. A part of MIT had always defined itself in opposition to the other heavyweight elite schools, especially Harvard. Perhaps MIT offered something different, something closer to what I was looking for. When I investigated further, I discovered that MIT offered a PhD in innovation. *Isn't that the act of thinking differently?* I thought. *Isn't that the essence of what I'm seeking? Isn't that really a process by which I can learn to be a generalist?* I enjoyed the self-contradiction of this challenge: to focus narrowly and go deep in a subject that is inherently broad. Was it possible that I could learn a skill set that I could apply to a broad range of real-world problems by narrowly focusing on this one idea? Yeah, I thought, *this is something I could really sink my teeth into.* And that was the big aha moment for me.

The more I thought about it, the more excited I got about this intellectual pursuit. Innovation promised a method of seeking answers to questions I'd long had. How does one learn to think critically in new ways? How does one develop the raw skills of knowledge generation, knowledge critiquing, figuring out what is possible? Those all traced back at least to my twelve-year-old participation in the Mini-Invention Innovation Team contest. But Blair and Yale had led me to yet more questions. What is true? What is opinion? What is fact? What is random occurrence? All of these questions point to uncertainty.

It was becoming clear to me that *all* opportunities emerge from environments of uncertainty—where lots of questions are asked and many possible answers are explored. In fact, I came to recognize that a lack of uncertainty often implies an absence of opportunity. As such, I realized I would have to become an expert at navigating uncertainty. The moment I understood this and accepted it, my behavior began to shift; my confidence began to rise. It would be many years before I would call myself a fox among hedgehogs, but I believe this is the time in my life when I started to behave like a fox. I was, in virtually every way, becoming a generalist. I was starting to see that one's behavior during life's most uncertain moments becomes the path forward. This insight would change everything.

My life arc from Landing, New Jersey, to Cambridge, Massachusetts, had taught me that knowledge is not static. It evolves. It is a construct of time and human interaction with that knowledge. What the research floor discovered on Friday became what the trading floor knew on Monday. But I was also becoming aware of a need to understand the truths that anchored this knowledge continuum—whether moral obligations, laws of nature, or matters of law.

What would be the principles that would inform my curiosity and decision-making? The commitment to open exploration itself, the migrant mindset, and a both-and approach to knowledge were becoming important guiding principles. But because of the wisdom passed down to me by my parents, I understood that my anchors would be as important as the knowledge itself. While staying true to my "North Star," I would need to learn how to create ideas, generate my own knowledge, and develop a process to effectively evaluate other people's knowledge (and anchors)—all would be necessary to truly innovate. What better place to do this, I thought, than in the hallowed halls of academia? This assumption would soon be put to the test.

CHAPTER 16

RATIONAL IRRATIONALITY

I sat in a room across the desk from an earnest woman who was utterly determined to be useful.

"So, Vikram," this MIT graduate school administrator asked, "what will your discipline be?"

I'd filled out applications, been accepted, and even secured grants for my education, so the question threw me. Equally determined to be useful, I replied, "I'm here to study innovation."

"Yes," she allowed. MIT understood that I was there for a PhD in innovation. "However," she continued, "which disciplinary field will be the foundation for your research?" Reading my confusion, she listed a menu of options. "Economics? Sociology? Political science?"

My answer threw her: "Yes!"

From day one, my interest in a large umbrella subject—innovation—was running headlong into academia's desire to pigeonhole. The faculty and administration assumed (and why wouldn't they?) that a PhD candidate was there to eventually pursue a career as an academic. After all, that is what more than 90 percent of their PhD students did. For better or worse, that meant training a graduate student to speak to, read, follow, and contribute to one specific tribe of researchers. Each discipline was siloed in its own department, often in its own building. The economists ruled their roost, the sociologists theirs, and so on. Once the MIT administrators knew my tribe of preference, the experts with whom I would work after graduation, they could be more helpful. Except my stated interest was not to pick any one tribe but rather to integrate many.

Those early meetings with MIT administrators all ended similarly. They allowed that eventually, I would have to declare my discipline, and I allowed that beyond innovation, I didn't intend to. The result was a truce of sorts. MIT was prepared to await my landing on an area of specialty, and I set out to enjoy all that MIT had to offer.

The result was that my return to academia was invigorating but also frustrating. My interest in a doctorate arose out of my desire to learn a cross-discipline work ethic focused on how to *create* ideas, how to *generate* knowledge. I had spent years doing analytical work in the "real world" of business, and many of the folks with whom I'd worked on Wall Street were good consumers of ideas. I wanted to be a producer of ideas. My goal wasn't to discover an idea that would impress a particular tribe of academics but to discover a good idea, an insight that might prove useful in the real world. The point of the PhD (at least to me) was to be trained in identifying the good ideas, master critical thinking, and if an idea held up under analysis, learn how to present it persuasively. I wanted to learn how to think for myself!

My degree was going to focus on innovation amid uncertain markets and supply chains, different industry fundamentals, and global finances and geopolitics. To me, it was a small step from this to my long-standing interests in geopolitics and national security and, of course, my interests in China, the Chinese military, and the strategies of the Chinese Communist Party, all areas that I'd worked on in the past. I wanted to use my time at the university to dig into these subjects as a function of my interest in navigating uncertainty. So, I had applied (simultaneously with my PhD application) to the Security Studies Program at MIT, with encouragement from two of my undergraduate mentors, Paul Kennedy and Paul Bracken.

Two comedies of errors quickly emerged. The first, nonconsequential, was the applause I received from my friends in finance.

This, however, was because when they heard "security studies," they assumed I was studying "securities," such as stocks and bonds, not national security. More consequential were the objections of MIT administrators. My view was that broadening my expertise into global security (and China) could only strengthen my work in innovation, and vice versa, but the administrators saw it differently. Their view was simple and emphatic. It boiled down to the flat assertion that a person couldn't be in a master's program in security studies *and* in a PhD program in innovation at the same time. Why? Their answer boiled down to "It just isn't done."

I decided to approach the problem differently.

I like to think my solution was . . . well, innovative. I ignored the administrators and simply signed up for the courses I wanted to take. The result was that during the first year of my PhD program, every class I took involved security studies. It turned out that the MIT administrators who had such strong opinions about what I could and could not study were considerably less interested in keeping track of which classes I actually took. By September 2003, or the end of my first year, I'd fulfilled all of the requirements for the master of science degree in political science through the Security Studies Program, including a paper that I converted into a master's thesis about how the US Coast Guard attempted to strategically innovate (using contractors) to secure larger budgets and get bigger boats. I also took a couple of classes that had broad relevance to economics and innovation.

By February of 2004, MIT had no choice but to award me a master of science degree in political science (security studies). How could they deny it when I'd been accepted to the program and done the work? However put out, the administrators then pointed out the consequence: I was behind on my PhD coursework. But this, too, had an obvious solution: get caught up. It was intense, but I was able to get it all done, and I successfully sat for my general exam, a threshold event in the life of a PhD student, by the summer of 2004. When it is deemed you are "done" with coursework, a committee of faculty convenes to grill you for a period of time to make sure you understand your field of study's "literature" (i.e., prior research). I was grilled, passed, and became what is colloquially known as "ABD" (all-but-dissertation) student. I still needed to write and defend a dissertation, but the degree in security studies hadn't slowed me down.

One reason I was able to accomplish this was because I treated my PhD program like a job. This was a very different approach from that taken by many of my peers. After classes were over, the students who were just out of undergrad would frequently go to bars, or the movies, or hang out with their friends. Those were all nonstarters for me. How could I do any of that when Kristen was working all day (and often late into the night) for her corporate law firm, Ropes & Gray? So I treated each day like a workday. When Kristen left home at eight o'clock to go to work, I walked out the door with her to go to MIT. If the weather cooperated, I would walk across Longfellow Bridge, which connected Boston's Beacon Hill to high-tech Cambridge. When the weather didn't, I hopped on the Red Line from the Charles/MGH stop to Kendall/MIT.

PhD students shared offices, and the one I was assigned to was, I believe, an old photocopy room that had been "converted," which seemed only to require the removal of a large Xerox machine. It had no windows, just four walls painted institutional white. I shared it with two other doctoral students, and it honestly felt more like a prison cell. As a result, I took to studying in the library and would regularly fill my backpack with all the necessary books and papers so that I was prepared to settle into the first available free chair. Occasionally, I would work in the lobby of the Cambridge Marriott, which had a Starbucks in it and great, free Wi-Fi.

Regardless, my day began by 8:30 a.m. and always entailed reading and analyzing research papers, preparing for and attending class, drafting papers and chapters, and then planning the remaining research to plug holes in what I didn't know. To get it done, I developed a routine that made me very productive. The touchstone of it was a trivial but extraordinarily effective tool that kept me on task:

I would use a note card to list what I wanted to do each day. And I wouldn't head home till I had crossed everything off and prepared my list for the following day.

By five or six at night, or about when my classmates would often leave to go out for a drink, I'd head home to have dinner with Kristen—unless she was working late, which meant I was, too.

It was this approach and that routine that encouraged me to pursue a second master's degree, this time from the MIT Sloan School of Management. Sloan is a first-class business school with top talent, but I also saw the degree as a hedged bet. The fact was, after I completed my general examination and was officially "ABD," I was not convinced that I wanted to complete the work necessary to earn the doctorate. It wasn't the workload; I had mastered that. It was that, unlike my peers, I had a hard time imagining a professional life in which I would mostly teach and write academic articles.

Kristen was almost alone in hearing my doubts. Until I made up my mind, I did not want to further confuse the MIT administrators. More pressing was not worrying my parents. They were thrilled that Kristen had pursued a respectable profession. She had acquired a skill and obtained a prestigious job at a world-class law firm. They were puzzled by me. They understood that however long I might take and whichever circuitous path I might follow, it increasingly appeared that I would end up in a "good" job. And of course, given their deep faith in education and its empowering qualities, they couldn't muster anything but pride that their son was a graduate student at MIT. They privately hoped this might turn me into an engineer but were prepared to accept me as a professor.

Everyone's difficulty with figuring out what I planned to be was compounded by my own ambivalence. The irony wasn't lost on me. I'd gone to MIT to study complexity so that I could better navigate uncertainty. Rather than pointing to a particular profession, such a skill seemed requisite for every profession. Though I was only slightly aware of it at the time, deciding what to do became my first real-life exercise in learning the habits of a professional generalist.

The first thing I realized was that the experts surrounding me—the faculty, administrative staff, and my fellow grad students—had a great deal of knowledge but only knew how to apply that knowledge in a narrow way. That was what toiling within the industry of academia required, and I remained uninterested. Among my reasons was that most of the junior faculty members I knew weren't happy. The pressure to publish weighed heavily on them. Securing tenure was the holy grail, and without it, young academics could expect a transient existence. Many of the academics I knew were moving, not across town but across the country, on a semiregular basis due to the shifting nature of opportunities. Such a fate would regularly disrupt Kristen's career. I admired many of MIT's faculty, benefited from their work, and knew that advice to follow in their footsteps was a nonstarter for me.

So I turned to a different sort of expert and complained.

One day in the late spring of 2004, upon successfully passing my general exam, or about two years into my PhD program, I called up David Swensen, one of my mentors at Yale, and confessed, "I've made a massive mistake. Academia's not for me. These people hide in their offices; they write anonymous reviews of the work of the people down the hallway about topics that nobody cares about. Why would I want to be one of these people? I think I'm wasting my life."

David, then the legendary chief investment officer at Yale, calmed me down. "I have a PhD, Vikram, and I'm running an endowment," he told me. "Other people have PhDs, and they do other things. It's not the end-all, be-all of a doctorate that you have to end up in academia."

"Yeah, but then why am I getting it?" I responded. Before he could answer, I laid out my reasoning. Sure, with a PhD, I could do many things, but I could do many things *without* a PhD. "There's no reason to get it, then," I concluded, repeating for good measure, "I'm wasting my time!"

"What would you rather be doing?" David's direct, simple question was clarifying.

"I want to do less abstract work," I said. And just as quickly, I added, "I want to apply what I'm learning."

"I tell you what. You like finance. Why don't we get you back into the world of finance for a summer internship?" Afterward, he connected me with Seth Klarman, who runs the Baupost Group, an investment firm based in Boston. Seth is a legendary investor. He was well known then, but today, he is spoken of in the same terms as Warren Buffett. Seth was kind enough to meet with me, and after we spoke for a while, he and his team asked if I'd work on some projects for the firm.

CHAPTER 17

A BUDDING PRACADEMIC

I spent the summer after my second year in the PhD program working for the Baupost Group, and I was reinvigorated. It was a welcome break after the deep dive into the innovation esoterica that led to my successfully passing my general exam. Baupost kept me on as a consultant in the fall, allowing me to help Doug Suliman, the chairman of one of the firm's portfolio companies and an outstanding executive who has grown into one of my closest friends and mentors—and someone from whom I continue to seek guidance and advice to this day. I juggled these responsibilities while I worked, albeit slowly and without my normal dedication, on my dissertation. The experience convinced me of one thing: by the time the Baupost consulting gig wrapped up in 2005, I knew I wasn't going to be an academic. I had a foot back in the professional investing world, and I wanted to keep it there. My explicit intent was to be both-and: both a student tracking toward his PhD and a research analyst studying how to invest differently.

Doors opened once I gave room and voice to the ambition. Because of my long-standing interest in global affairs, a friend of a friend connected me in 2005 to Oechsle International Advisors, an investment management firm with billions under management. One of the company's founders, Dee Keesler, I discovered, was running a global hedge fund that was able to invest anywhere in the world and in any sector. I was intrigued and recognized the opportunity as one that would allow me to be a global generalist.

The hedge fund seemed to be an ideal fit for me, and fortunately, Dee needed someone to help with research on investment opportunities around the world and across industries. Not just balance sheets and reported figures but more in-depth research, requiring the integration of multiple perspectives. The job, basically, would be to go visit companies, meet CEOs and senior leaders, attend industry conferences, and learn about which companies were thriving and which were struggling. Then I'd value the companies and make investment recommendations about whether we should buy a particular company's stock (i.e., go long) or bet against it (i.e., go short). It sounded awesome, a perfect fit for my both-and generalist instincts and global explorer interests. I'd get to travel again and learn more about businesses and how they operated all over the world. It had been a long time since I'd scratched this itch. So I took that position while I continued to work (with consistent, albeit not very intense, effort) toward the completion of my PhD.

There were lots of invigorating aspects of working on the fund, among them being sent overseas to conduct on-the-ground research. This was the opposite of sitting in a library and reading other people's articles about yet other people's scholarship. In one instance, I flew to Jakarta, Indonesia, to study the fundamentals of several commodity and consumer companies. Indonesia is a vibrant country of more than 280 million people, of which nearly 90 percent are Muslim. It just so happened that my visit fell one week after a Dutch newspaper published a cartoon depicting, and making fun of, the prophet Mohammed. It was provocative, a deliberate insult to practicing Muslims. Half a world away from Holland, my driver rounded a corner and stopped in front of a mob turning over cars and vandalizing anything that looked Western. Whether or not this mob would decide I looked like the American I was seemed a risk not worth taking. I exited the car and got myself somewhere safe.

On the flight home from that trip, I couldn't help but connect the risks and uncertainty of investing in the world's fourth-most-populous nation with the enormous opportunities Indonesia presented to the investment community. It wasn't the first time—or the last—that I was struck by the tight connection between uncertainty and opportunity.

My real-life experience during the years finishing my graduate work at MIT kept confirming my intuition that although others held out hope I would eventually land on a straight, short path to a narrow specialty, I found ever-richer rewards by steadfastly refusing to. It's probably why I identify with the oft-quoted saying, "Not all who wander are lost."

Outside of MIT, I found it natural to connect the dots from Swensen to Klarman to Oechsle. Within MIT, I found it natural to connect the dots across the silos of academic approaches. To my degree in security studies, I had added another from MIT's Sloan School of Management. These two interests—security and management—allowed me to undertake a deep dive into defense innovation, or rapid adaptations driven by existential threats such as the Soviet Union. This quickly connected to the emergence of the technology sector because, as Andy Grove noted in his similarly titled book, "Only the paranoid survive." Competitive forces mattered, irrespective of domain.

Likewise, it seemed obvious to me that psychology mattered in decision-making in a way that traditional economic theory failed to incorporate. This was before behavioral economics was a common buzzword and when "*Homo economicus*," the average consumer, was presumed to be a hyperrational, always-optimizing robot, constantly calculating costs and benefits. Of course, the moment you investigated fields other than economics—from history to, most obviously, psychology—you realized that life was messier and that many people made suboptimal decisions for all kinds of reasons. A result could be that a large population of well-intentioned individuals might drive their country—and with it, the economy—off a cliff. This was crystal clear to me, not only from reading broadly but also from watching the implosion of the Japanese bubble as an intern at Bear Stearns. Traders had panicked both as the bubble inflated and then again when it burst. Necessary to navigating uncertainty was to factor in a certain amount of irrationality.

Before I arrived at MIT, I was an admirer of Yale economist Bob Shiller's thought-provoking book *Irrational Exuberance*. The first edition, published in the fall of 2000, had warned that the valuation of tech companies, which rose sharply during the dot-com boom of the late 1990s, was much too high and due for a brutal correction. Amid the prevailing market optimism of that time, Shiller's analysis was dismissed by many. After all, they said, Shiller had been writing similar warnings for years. But he ended up looking like a genius when his book hit the shelves at virtually the same time as the tech bubble burst. I counted myself among the impressed and was eager to read the revised edition of *Irrational Exuberance* published in 2005. It began with a new chapter that discussed concerning dynamics driving the US housing market.

Shiller was a card-carrying economist who also seemed to think for himself, and as such, I identified with his approach. Unlike most economic books on bubbles, which focus on the divergence between values and prices, Shiller included concepts such as information cascades and how ideas spread. He was drawing from different disciplines, connecting different dots, and reaching different conclusions. It was refreshing to read.

In the second edition, published in early 2005, Shiller showed how housing prices in the United States, which had mostly been in synch with inflation for more than a hundred years, had risen steeply after the bursting of the technology bubble. Why was this happening? Shiller methodically walked readers through the probable causes, breaking down in detail all the factors that might lead to higher real estate costs. Was it the price of materials? No, they had stayed the same. The cost of labor? Nope. Population as a proxy for demand? Nope. All the relevant economic factors that usually affected the pricing of houses were stable. All signs, Shiller warned, pointed to a speculative bubble in housing, spurred in part by lower interest rates. A major part of the US economy was booming, and despite the assurances from policymakers and experts alike that there had never been nor would ever be a nationwide housing bubble, Shiller implied the current housing-market exuberance was, in fact, irrational.

I'll never forget the sense of unease I felt as I parsed the graphs and copious data Shiller had assembled to lay out his argument for a rising housing bubble. It was a master class in first-principles thinking. Abandoning most of the assumptions economists had built their discipline on, the revealed preferences of optimizing markets efficiently captured in "correct" prices, Shiller was able to spot a bubble before it burst. Because of my experience in finance, Shiller's argument made a lot of sense to me. But as had been the case with his predictions about the tech bubble, many financial experts were accusing Shiller of being an alarmist. Despite centuries of data to the contrary, economists don't like to think that the market behaves in irrational ways—at least not at this scale. Even after the collapse of the tech boom, there was an enormous amount of faith in the stability of the economy and the regulatory mechanisms that had evolved over time to stabilize the housing market.

I didn't have such faith and was convinced that dark clouds were gathering on the horizon. The question, of course, was what, if anything, to do about it.

CHAPTER 18

INSIGHT TO ACTION

I was so persuaded by Shiller's argument that when I got back to our apartment on Beacon Hill, I immediately explained to Kristen what I'd read.

She listened. She went through the data and the argument. She'd long had an interest in real estate and the housing market and quickly understood the point Shiller was making. We reached a common agreement about what to do with our small condominium apartment.

"We need to list it today," we said, almost in unison. I added, "I'm going to call a broker."

Kristen scoffed. She already had a real estate license. Always enterprising, Kristen had earned the license while in law school. It was less that I had forgotten the fact than I had assumed she was busy. And wouldn't a broker help our apartment command top offers?

"Why give our money to someone else when we can do it ourselves?" was Kristen's first response. Her second arose right out of Shiller's argument: "If we're selling during a still-inflating bubble, we should be able to get a good price on our own."

I couldn't argue with her logic and was grateful for her willingness to find the time. The result? We sold our apartment near the top of the market during the summer of 2005. Sure, we were a bit early, but that was far better than being a little late. (The market effectively peaked during the summer of 2007 but had plateaued from 2005 to 2007.) Friends and family had two years to question and chuckle over our decision and the "irrationality" of our process—until Shiller's second big prediction came true when the housing market crashed in 2008.

In the immediate moment, I felt urgency and clarity. It was less that Shiller had provided me with a crystal ball than he had presented me with a wealth of data and an interpretation of it that I could stack against other data, other interpretations. Succinctly: I concluded Shiller was the more persuasive and acted accordingly. Only in retrospect did I wonder why so many experts missed the (now) obvious warning signs. I wasn't privy to anything unavailable to them. I had been a student of markets and valuations for far fewer years than many, many others. And it wasn't as if I'd stayed on the sidelines during the housing bull market. I'd bought that condo on Beacon Hill, after all. It was also not accidental that I was pursuing a doctorate in innovation precisely because of my interest in uncertainty and how to navigate it. It was less that I was more attuned to the possibility of sudden economic shocks than many of my peers than it was that, unlike my peers, I was connecting different and more of the proverbial dots.

Some of those dots were from personal experience.

My experience growing up in a lower-middle-class family of immigrants made me more aware of how precarious and uncertain life could be. My father had lived through the sudden upheaval of geopolitical uncertainty when the British Empire retreated from India. He knew that a smaller boat feels the dips and swells of rough waters much more than a large ship. Watching the Japanese bubble burst as an intern at Bear Stearns taught me that in rough enough waters, even a large ship will go down. Hell, the housing-market crash came uncomfortably close to swamping the global economy. All my life, I'd seen how elites had the luxury of navigating the unsteady seas of the economy in relative safety. This can create a false sense of security when a tidal wave approaches.

Shiller taught me that sometimes, decisions need to be made from a vantage point of rational irrationality.

Of course, selling our home created a new problem. Where were we going to live? We already had a place in Maine, and I suggested we could make that our base of operations—it was only a seventy-mile drive to Boston. Then I came up with another idea: Why don't we live in a hotel in Boston for part of the time? I had done so while working for Booz Allen, and doing so with Kristen promised to be much more enjoyable! And so we did, commuting into the city from Wells, Maine, a few days a week and staying in hotels two or three nights a week—and more if work demanded more from us. Indeed, the more we learned the rules of guest awards, the more comfortable we were able to be. If this seems like a luxurious lifestyle, it was also the most economical. Purchase hotel stays in bulk, and they are sold at a discount; accumulate stays at a hotel—even discounted stays—and you accumulate status, points, and lots of perks.

Life was fun and frivolous, and with our student loans paid off, Kristen and I were beginning to enjoy eating out and even attending an occasional show. And amid this joyous and fun lifestyle, Kristen and I were soon ecstatic to learn that she was pregnant. It was an exciting time, and we continued to enjoy a relatively relaxed existence. Eventually, Mike Bender, one of my more live-and-let-live and carefree friends from Yale who had served as a groomsman in our wedding, called and suggested the "Royal Mansharamanis" really shouldn't have a newborn living in a hotel. Hearing it from him was a message I couldn't ignore. But it was 2006, and of course, I wasn't about to jump back into owning real estate because the bubble I saw coming hadn't yet burst. Kristen, sharing my conviction, agreed, and we soon rented an apartment in the Coolidge Corner neighborhood of Brookline, slightly outside of Boston.

Far from setting me back, the extra burden of holding down a day job; living with Kristen, who was ever more visibly pregnant; living off campus; and completing my remaining graduate work made me more productive than ever. By the fall of '06, four years after I started my PhD, I had written and was ready to defend my thesis. MIT, however, disagreed. Administrators in the department told me, "You're not ready. You haven't published anything. You don't have a job-market paper. You're not yet good to go."

I had no patience for this institutional inertia, however well intended. My immense productivity in the last year of my PhD program wasn't entirely due to my enthusiasm for completing the degree. The truth was, I was working on a tight, fixed deadline. My race to complete my degree was measurable in Kristen's pregnancy. If getting across the PhD finish line was going to be hard while working a job, I knew it was going to be orders of magnitude more difficult with a newborn. And more than that, Kristen and I wanted to be active parents, engaged in all aspects of our children's lives. This meant I had to finish my degree, because Kristen would likely exit the legal rat race.

So I pushed back. "I'm not saying you have to approve my dissertation," I argued. "If my defense isn't good enough, the faculty can and should reject my work. But you shouldn't deny me the chance to defend my work." As the situation escalated, I got others involved, and finally, it was agreed to schedule the all-important, make-or-break meeting. At that point, I knew the battle was basically over. This was the flip side of obstructions made of straw. Once you're determined to resist them, they crumble. Faculty members rarely fail people at the stage of their studies when they're defending their work.

Long story short, Victoria Teresa Mansharamani ("Tori") was born in June 2006, and I successfully defended my work in December of that year. The following February, I received my doctorate. Given the graduation cycle, however, it wasn't until June 2007 that I was able to walk across a stage—an event that young Tori, Kristen, my parents, and my sister were able to see in person.

I was damn proud. I had done the work. It was good. No, I didn't do the academic job talk. No, I didn't publish the academic papers. But I did what I needed in order to earn the degree. And starting in 2007, I had earned the right to insert *Dr.* ahead of my name.

My closest friends called, jokingly, to describe their medical ailments. I replied that I couldn't help their aches and pains, but I was game if they wanted to meet in Vegas. My thesis was about the gaming industry, and I'd studied how casino companies such as Harrah's Entertainment had used lots of data about customers to treat each of them differently. What had held my fascination was that these companies, whose business model boiled down to making money from the predictable uncertainty of craps tables, card games, and roulette wheels, were skilled at collecting lots and lots of data about their customers and then using that data to customize the experience of millions of guests who came through their doors in a way that increased loyalty and profits. I didn't know it at the time, but I was writing about the power of big data before anyone was talking about "big data." (The dissertation is publicly available via MIT's libraries, and you can find it if you'd like. It is titled "Scale and Differentiation in Services.")

Swensen's assurances notwithstanding, most of the world responded to Dr. Vikram Mansharamani by presuming I was bound for a university. It was active work to convince them otherwise. What didn't help was telling them I had a migrant mindset or had gone to MIT to be trained at being both-and—or even that my focus was learning how to innovate in the face of complex uncertainties. I grew increasingly frustrated that the answer that made the most sense to me—"I got the degree to become a better generalist"—made little sense to anyone else. Those who knew me well started calling me a "pracademic," a shorthand way to describe the apparently oxymoronic but accurate label of having become a "practical academic."

Fortunately, to most of the world, announcing you had a PhD from MIT was a full stop. That I knew I had a PhD in being a generalist could be more of a private insight than a public declaration.

And business colleagues cared less about labels than did academics. It made sense to them that the multiple-lens approach I had learned could be applied to everything from gambling in Las Vegas to boom-bust investment cycles on Wall Street. It had broad applicability across industries. That is certainly what my colleagues at Oechsle understood.

Four years and four months after starting at MIT, I had two master's degrees and a PhD. And I already had a job. It felt good. I was working at a global fund, traveling around the world and meeting with investors, corporate leaders, government officials, the occasional academic, and even journalists. I had spent time on the ground in dozens and dozens of countries including China, Russia, South Africa, Norway, Thailand Brazil, India, and Canada. I was living the generalist existence I had fought to create. Kristen had a bright future in law. We had a beautiful new daughter. Our ducks were very much in a row, our trajectory predictable. But of course, life is never completely predictable, as Kristen and I were soon to learn.

CHAPTER 19

TOSSING AND TURNING

Being type A individuals, Kristen and I didn't want to leave anything about parenting to chance. We read books, visited expert websites, and debated the benefits of Weissbluth versus Ferber in sleep training. Pediatricians were advisers, but we had trouble relying on single sources of input. Our parents guided, but we were strong-willed. It was a whirlwind—one that we, like many parents, did our best to navigate. We coped. But we also noticed that Tori didn't fit most of the descriptions we had read about infants.

Early on, we sensed that Tori was having developmental issues. She struggled with feeding, and we often found ourselves distracting her so she would ingest the appropriate nourishment to develop. As a young toddler, she seemed to struggle with basic coordination and tasks involving body awareness. The doctors we consulted, however, did not seem to be concerned. They also voiced no consensus, though each voiced her or his opinion with the utmost confidence. This left us, already insecure new parents, constantly second-guessing our parenting as we saw Tori struggling. What were we doing wrong? Kristen decided to leave her demanding job as a litigator at Ropes & Gray so that she could spend more time with Tori and figure out how best to care for her.

For Kristen, this didn't translate into just more time at home. She is nothing if not entrepreneurial. No longer working at the law firm, she needed a new outlet for her energy, creativity, and desire to be a present parent and improve her community and the world in which we lived. For this reason, in 2008, not long after leaving her law firm, she decided to start a Montessori school in Boston. This was partly inspired by her own background: Kristen had been educated in a Montessori school and had benefited from the freedom and creativity of that educational approach. But more importantly, she felt it might serve Tori well. She wanted to expose Tori to foreign languages, music, and the arts. She wanted to place her in a curriculum that was adaptive, not conformist. Additionally, she wanted to make the same opportunity available to others. And so, in the fall of 2008, after months and months of juggling parenting with business planning, as colleagues and I watched yet another financial bubble burst, Kristen opened the doors at the Torit Montessori School (named after Tori, the additional *T* being her middle initial).

This was an extraordinary accomplishment. I helped when and as I could, but my job required jumping on planes and assessing international corporations. This meant Kristen was caring for Tori full-time while setting up a business. In one humorous situation, Kristen had two-year-old Tori with her while interviewing a Chinese language instructor. Juggling tasks, at one point, she asked the candidate to engage Tori while she addressed a pressing matter. Keeping the attention of a two-year-old is no trivial undertaking. It requires a dynamism and energy atypical in almost any job other than teaching. It turned out that this very reserved candidate couldn't keep our daughter's attention. Her candidacy was dashed by Tori repeating, "Bye-bye . . . okay, bye-bye."

I remain impressed by Kristen's ability to multitask and get the best out of people, even recruiting Tori to help evaluate candidates!

The best thing about starting your own school is that you get to set the curriculum, and Kristen had strong ideas about the values she wanted to teach. We both understood that the world was growing ever smaller and more interconnected, so if we wanted to prepare the next generation to thrive in that world, they needed to understand the diversity and complexity of humanity. In addition to revitalizing a sense of civic responsibility, Kristen wanted to expose students to foreign cultures, traditions, and languages. This was never more important than in those years after 9/11, when xenophobia in the United States was running high against Arabic speakers and Muslims and even people like the Sikhs, who were not even remotely connected to the Middle East or the 9/11 terrorists.

To address the ignorance that can lead to stereotyping, Torit's curriculum exposes students to foreign speakers and books at a very early age and celebrates a variety of holidays and cultural traditions. Not just Christmas but everything from Eid to Diwali to Chinese New Year. At the time of this writing, more than 100 families educate their children at the school Kristen built. A testament to Kristen's perseverance, managerial talents, entrepreneurial spirit, and commitment to education, Torit grew into a beacon of civic engagement and empowerment. To this day, I remain super proud of her and her achievements.

As Kristen was busy preparing for and launching Torit, I was working full-time to navigate my own career uncertainty. What I had missed was that anticipating uncertain markets and irrational economic forces was one thing, but anticipating competing visions and egos in investment management was something else altogether.

Even as the global economy teeter-tottered ever closer to the financial brink, the team I was part of at Oechsle dissolved, with its two principals going in separate directions. One was able to immediately launch a new firm (specializing in Asian investments) and offered to hire me. Because of noncompete language in the other principal's employment agreements, he would have to wait for some time before he could launch his own firm. He suggested there would likely be a role for me when it launched, and this appealed to me because I wanted to continue working as a global generalist. But I also needed an income, and honesty and integrity meant admitting this. So I accepted the job to work for the firm focused on Asian markets, even as I waited to see if Dee would launch a new global fund.

Things came to a head in the fall of 2007. Perhaps anticipating that the other firm might soon be formed, the company employing me insisted I sign a long-term employment agreement. This would have tied my hands, and I said, "No, thank you." When I declined, I was immediately fired.

Despite this unexpected twist in life, I was confident in my prospects. Yes, the global generalist firm was still a concept, an idea that had not yet been made into reality. Yes, storm clouds were gathering, if not opening up on, global financial markets. Of course, there was stress—how could there not be?—but I remained upbeat and was convinced I'd be back at work soon, and I still had plenty to do.

I also decided to use the break to visit former colleagues and friends from Merrill Lynch and Bear Stearns in New York. Like all of Wall Street, these frontline financial companies were facing mounting challenges. As I crisscrossed Manhattan in late 2007, how bad things would get was just one of a mounting list of unknowns. A given was that when the music stopped, there would be fewer seats for those still standing. Everyone was working long hours, which translated into a few missed meetings. At the meetings that did take place, I saw again and again exceedingly talented individuals who had spent years in lucrative, illustrious jobs now scrambling to respond to the overwhelming uncertainty and the possibility of a forthcoming financial tsunami. No doubt, there was genius at all of these Wall Street firms, but too much of it was too siloed, too narrowly focused, and consequently too late to anticipate and act collectively. Just months after that trip, Bear Stearns, the storied firm where I had first learned the basics of the business, would fail. And later in 2008, so, too, would Lehman Brothers, its bankruptcy setting off an international banking crisis.

Despite it all, I felt on top of the forces pushing and pulling my world. Because we'd read the tea leaves back in 2005 and sold our apartment, we still had savings. And unlike many of my friends and colleagues who had gone directly from undergrad to finance, I had spent years training to live with complexity, to navigate uncertainty.

Hell, I held a doctorate degree in the subject! My confidence lasted until I returned to Boston.

That evening, Kristen and I noticed that Tori was gagging, but only occasionally. We couldn't tell why. She was crawling around the apartment but would sometimes grab her throat in discomfort, and when given water or food, she would gag. No surprise, but we were concerned and promptly sped off to Boston Children's Hospital, which was only a few miles from our apartment in Brookline. And there we sat in the emergency room, helpless while our poor daughter suffered, waiting until someone could help. An hour later, we finally got to see a nurse who looked Tori over and suggested there was something stuck in her throat. A quick X-ray revealed that she was right—she had swallowed a penny. It wasn't completely blocking her airway but obstructing it enough that it made it difficult for her to swallow and breathe.

We were horrified. When Tori had started complaining, our first instinct had been to give her food—a small piece of carrot. To new parents, her behavior had all the hallmarks of an infant who was hungry. We now realized that if we'd kept trying to feed her, she could easily have choked to death! Fortunately, the hospital was able to immediately perform a procedure to remove the obstruction.

After the relief of identifying the problem and having it addressed came the doubt and fear. Tori was barely over a year old, and we'd almost killed her. These are the days that get seared into your memory as a parent. Once we got Tori home, we threw sleep training aside. She was sleeping in our room that night. That evening, I tossed and turned. The last twenty-four hours had been a rattling end to a difficult twelve months.

CHAPTER 20

Academic Bubbles

The first decade of my professional life had twists and turns and ups and downs, and it was marked by navigating the cross-currents of graduate school, professional opportunities, and starting a family. And while I'd had a healthy dose of challenges, the generalist in me was developing a philosophy around the fact that every perspective was limited and incomplete. As a result, I often tried to tap into the thinking of others, those who might reflect on my experiences from a different vantage point. One person who selflessly listened and helped my thinking was David Swensen.

Amid all the demands of home and work, I relished every chance I had to play squash with David. At the time, our friendship centered mostly around these fun—but still intense—matches. Afterward, during our cool-down bottles of water and lunch at Mory's, we'd discuss what was going on in our lives. He was an invaluable mentor, advising me through the many unexpected transitions and life changes I was dealing with, and I always paid close attention to what he had to say. So I was surprised when, in the middle of a game, he pulled me aside to offer some unexpected advice: "Vikram," he said to me, "you have a PhD now. You should teach."

Wasn't this the guy who had talked me into completing the doctorate *because* it didn't mean a life in academia? And David had been on the receiving end of no small number of my speeches about all that was wrong with higher education. Why on earth would I want to become a part of a university?

"How can I teach," I asked him, "if I don't want to be an academic?"

David assured me there were plenty of teaching roles available that didn't require submitting to the petty departmental politics and nightmarish administrative bureaucracy that stifle higher education. Instead, he encouraged me to think about it from another perspective. What did the world need to know? What knowledge could I impart to students? What did I want to teach?

This was in early 2008, as the signs of the coming housing crash were all around us. Bubbles were very much in the public conversation, even though they were largely misunderstood. Shiller's insights into economic behavior had made him an author of multiple bestsellers but hadn't materially dented the way economics was taught or practiced on campuses. And it would be three years before Daniel Kahneman's *Thinking, Fast and Slow* would make the insights of behavioral economics kitchen-table buzzwords. Still, there were interesting first-principle thinkers out there with new insights, if you were willing to connect the dots. A few economists in the mold of Shiller warned that irrationality and randomness governed the markets. Some psychologists, led by Kahneman, cited research to show that humans were implicitly biased and not optimizing decision-makers. Legal scholars, such as Cass Sunstein, accepted Kahneman's conclusions and offered corporate and governmental "libertarian paternalism," though this seemed a fancy way of saying, "Experts know best." The missing piece, I was convinced, was the power of generalists to sustain broad attention to the insights of numerous experts; use multiple lenses to discover the most valuable ideas and opportunities; and after gathering and weighing knowledge, experience, and common sense, act by thinking for themselves.

By mid-2008, I had an answer to the question that David had posed: "I want to teach about bubbles."

Financial bubbles are case studies in badly navigated uncertainty. Yes, there were always a small number of people who had read the tea leaves accurately and acted. But the nature of a bust is that the majority of individuals and organizations (and often governments) hadn't. Most had thought narrowly, followed the explanations of the loudest voices, and embraced a herd mentality. One of the most common features of all bubbles, back to at least the infamous tulip mania of the 1630s (and likely before), is that a large majority of participants had failed to think for themselves. And ever since 2005, I had been convinced that we were living through yet another one.

Eventually, thanks to David's introductions, months after our initial conversation, I was able to get a job at Yale teaching a seminar on financial booms and busts. My initial foray into teaching was via the university's College Seminars Program, which allowed for a handful of multidisciplinary topics to be taught via courses that lived outside the departmental structure. It was a perfect fit for me and the topic of bubbles. My approach was simple: liberal arts meets finance. Multiple lenses. Economics, psychology, politics, sociology, swarm and herd dynamics, and so forth. Then, using concrete cases of bubbles past and recent, we would explore how these lenses came into play. It would all end in a culminating project in which students tried to identify the next big bubble. It was awesome to plan out and fun in practice. The students loved it, and the class was massively oversubscribed.

It was a grueling schedule. I was still helping to manage money in Boston—a full-time job—on top of the demands of helping to raise Tori with Kristen. On Mondays, I would work at the office until the markets closed and then make the two-hour drive from Boston to New Haven. After a quick bite to eat near campus, I'd teach the seminar from 7:00 to 9:00 p.m. Then, when the class was over, I'd grab a cup of coffee to keep me awake for the two-hour drive back home. The next morning, it would be back to the office before 8:00 a.m.

As draining as the long commutes were, I was living the life of a generalist in fact if not in name. A husband and father advising a fund making global investments, and a teacher of undergraduates. I was not just both-and; I was all of the above.

Uncertainty, from an overlooked penny to the irrational exuberance of global markets, was a constant element of life. Sitting in the hospital that night with Tori convinced me that it would be impossible to eliminate uncertainty—better, instead, I concluded, to accept its presence and navigate through it. All of my experiences to date suggested that a broad, dot-connecting, silo-crossing approach was likely the best way to navigate uncertainty. I needed to embrace the way of the fox; it was time to be a professional generalist.

CHAPTER 21

A Goddamn Tragedy

I was entering a series of years in which opportunity wasn't defined by what was presented but *what I decided to do* with whatever was presented. These were the years when I honed a practice, a way of choosing, that balanced being both an expert and a generalist. I was defining for myself what it meant to be a professional generalist.

Though Kristen and I had made some unconventional career moves up until that point, on paper, our life together was like that of a lot of the other couples we knew. We'd accumulated degrees from Yale, MIT, Harvard; I was a financial analyst and educator, and Kristen was a lawyer turned entrepreneur. We owned a nice condominium apartment in a pleasant suburb of Boston. We were ticking all the boxes. Then, I made a choice that, at the time, seemed inconsequential but would prove to be life-altering: I decided to write a book. I blame Charley Ellis.

I'd heard of Charley long before I got to know him as a friend. His sterling reputation preceded him. He is the founder of Greenwich Associates; the author of more than a dozen books, including the bestselling *Winning the Loser's Game*; the former chair of the storied Yale endowment; and a passionate advocate of passive investing. *Winning the Loser's Game* was an extended explanation of the findings he presented in his 1975 article "The Loser's Game." The article and book challenged the idea that financial experts could outperform the market. Both were backed up by research that was quantifiable, data rich, and highly persuasive. What Charley made transparent was that most professional money managers delivered results no better, and sometimes worse (often quite a bit worse), than index funds.

If an expert underperforms a passive, algorithm-guided fund, what is the expert's case for commanding a fee for his or her advice? Get to know Charley or read his work thoughtfully, and you realize that his argument wasn't anti-expert. Rather, it could be summarized as "Pay for actual expertise in fact." I hadn't crystallized the notion yet, but it was Charley and his goddamn tragedy that eventually led me to the insight that you have to keep experts on tap, not on top.

One lesson that has really sunk in as I've gotten older is that one's life can change profoundly in a moment, and one isn't always aware of when those moments are happening. What if I'd never secured the financial assistance to attend Blair? What if I'd ended up working for Enron? Going back farther, what if my father had decided to move to Canada or England instead of the United States? What if he'd never gotten on that boat to Mumbai? At times, it can seem like we're just balls on a pool table. We are hurtling through our lives, bumping into others, and sometimes affecting each other's trajectories in ways that are too complex to predict. That experience can cause us to seek out and rely on experts. Someone must be able to make better sense of this complexity!

Of course, we're not billiard balls. We have agency and control, and we can often influence our own choices. Rarely do we have complete control, and rarely do we want complete control. We have families, friends, neighbors, and colleagues to live among, and a wide world out there to live in and make something of. And one of those choices we make is whether, when our paths intersect with others, we are open to new possibilities and experiences . . . or not.

At the time, late in 2009, Kristen and I had again settled into a steady routine. I was working at SDK Capital, the global generalist fund that had relaunched after Dee's departure from Oechsle

International Advisors, and traveling globally, researching different foreign markets and companies for our investors. Kristen was managing the by-then-thriving Torit Montessori School. And we were both engaged in that other demanding job—being parents. Additionally, once a week, I would make the long commute to New Haven to teach my class at Yale, which had grown so popular that, to my dismay, I had to deny students the chance to take the course. Just as we were figuring out how to keep all these balls in the air, we found out, to our joy, that Kristen was pregnant again. Four years, apparently, was just enough time for us to forget the stress and exhaustion of introducing a baby into the house. Looking back on this chaotic period in our lives, it seems funny to me now that just when a reasonable choice would have been to retrench and focus, Charley approached me with a ridiculous idea.

By that point, I had known Charley since 1999, when David Swensen had introduced us at one of his (in)famous tailgate parties in New Haven. You see, each year, for either the Harvard–Yale or the Princeton–Yale football game (whichever happened to be in New Haven on that particular year), David and the Yale Investment Office would host a gathering at the Yale Bowl that offered beverages and food that exceeded the quality and quantity of that offered at student tailgates. He made a point of inviting all Yale alumni who were helping—directly or indirectly (as was my case as a young analyst working at Great Hill Partners in 1999)—to invest Yale's endowment. David was a gracious host, moving seamlessly between the young professionals and titans of Wall Street who made the annual pilgrimage to New Haven.

It was while we were in line for chili and cornbread during the fall of 2010 that Charley uttered the four words that changed my life: "It's a goddamn tragedy!"

Reading the confused look on my face, Charley repeated himself.

"It's a goddamn tragedy."

Stupefied, I pleaded ignorance. "I'm sorry, Charley, but I don't understand."

He paused and looked me in the eyes. "Only a handful of privileged Yale undergraduates are benefiting from your ideas." He took another bite, chewed, and swallowed. "It's a tragedy."

As one of the most intelligent men I knew, Charley was—and still is—an expert on experts. Throughout his numerous books, he'd made the case again and again that thinking and deciding for yourself meant assessing advice, expertise, and performance before following an expert's advice. As someone with a deep grasp of the history of finance, he always asked me what I was covering in my boom-bust course. And today, he had an idea to solve the "goddamn tragedy."

"Vikram, you have to write a book. Your ideas must be made available to others outside of our little privileged world."

Under normal circumstances, I would have seriously considered this advice from a good friend. But a book? I didn't have enough time for all the things I was already doing, *and* I had another kid on the way. I remember laughing, telling Charley, "You know, *you* write books. Maybe you should write it!" I offered to help, suggesting he could use my syllabus as a structure to organize it.

Perhaps Charley could see how frazzled I was, because he dropped the subject. Or so I thought. A few days later while driving between New Haven and Boston, however, I got a call from Bill Falloon, one of the many editors whom Charley has impressed. "I was talking to Charley," Bill told me after introducing himself, "and he told me you want to write a book. Is that right?"

"Well, not really. I mean, yes, Charley and I had spoken about a book, but—"

"Vikram, that's great! I think there's a need for a book like the one you're writing."

As I struggled to respond, I noticed that my speed had increased. I was now going almost eighty miles per hour, trying to cope with the conversation: "Bill . . . I'm not even sure where to begin here; I hadn't planned to—"

"It's no problem—I'll chip in to help you get this done. I've worked with several first-time authors. Let's plan to speak tomorrow.

I'll have some of my team jump on a call, and we'll get started. This will be great!"

The next day, Bill listened, prodded for more information, and offered advice, and the next thing I knew, I was converting my course syllabus into a proposal that would become my first book, *Boombustology: Spotting Financial Bubbles before They Burst*. With Bill's help, I was able to rapidly convert the material from my course into a coherent manuscript. Week 1 on the syllabus became Chapter 1; Week 2, Chapter 2. And Bill's guidance helped expand the scope of the message to one that was much improved because of his engagement and support.

To this day, I remain impressed by Charley's Jedi mind trick. Only a goddamn genius could turn a casual conversation in the chili-and-cornbread line into a published book. And how he made me feel like it was my idea, well, I never saw it coming.

CHAPTER 22

Chain Reactions

What I didn't anticipate was how Charley's nudge to publish a book would set off a chain reaction that completely changed my life's trajectory. His suggestion, backed up by Bill's encouragement, not only forced me to go deeper into the study of booms and busts but also spurred serious reflection about the purpose to which I'd been putting my knowledge. It wasn't so much a tragedy as a fact. I had been living an eventful life at home, in my narrow world of investment management, and in the classroom at Yale. In reality, my world was composed of Kristen and Tori, colleagues and clients, and finally, a couple dozen undergraduates. With a book, I could share my knowledge broadly. More importantly, I had to. Bill wanted a book that could reach wider audiences and readers who would find the book useful years after I wrote it.

The exercise of writing *Boombustology* for, and promoting it to, the general public forced me to think deeply about questions I'd mostly given only scant thought to. Why am I studying these subjects in the first place? Who is benefiting from my research? How can I help readers with the skills and knowledge I've acquired? Until this point, I had used those skills and knowledge to build a career and look after my family. Perhaps Charley was right. Maybe there was more that I could be doing. But just whether, and how,

I could turn Charley's "goddamn tragedy" into a triumph was the task ahead of me.

Earlier, David Swensen had shared war stories of writing his first book, *Pioneering Portfolio Management*. He noted that writing it was an exhausting process, especially given that he had a demanding day job and then wanted to spend time with his family in the evenings. He warned me that he often was forced to write at night. As is typical of young and ambitious professionals like me, I thought I would avoid such a fate. But when I finally sat down to write in my small office in our condo in Brookline, it was often after 10:00 p.m. Papers were piled across the floor, dozens of books opened and upside down on the precise page I needed to reference, and note cards were strewn about. I grew addicted to Diet Coke and found my weight rising. But I made progress, and by early 2011, shortly after Kristen and I welcomed Kai Elan Mansharamani into the world on November 28, 2010, I had a complete manuscript in hand!

In the end, the book built on the course syllabus, approaching the understanding of booms and busts through five lenses: microeconomics, macroeconomics, psychology, politics, and biology. It then discussed a series of famous historical bubbles through these different perspectives, such as Tulipomania in the Netherlands in the 1630s, the Great Depression, the Japanese bubble, the Asian financial crisis, and then the housing bust of 2008–2009.

Each of the cases demonstrated the power of multi-lens thinking. It was only by looking through multiple perspectives that one could grasp the magnitude of these bubbles, and more importantly, I felt, singular perspectives were inconsistent in delivering useful insights. Macroeconomics defined the Great Depression, but psychology helped define how each country responded. I was once again reminded that knowledge is not static and that the human behavior of many in times of high uncertainty is what shapes in-the-moment reactions along the knowledge continuum. Tulipomania was almost pure psychology, the original example of irrational exuberance, but the spark that ignited the bubble began with regulatory changes.

The 1997 Asian crisis was first and foremost about microeconomic decisions, but contagion and herd behavior quickly took the chaos global and ensnared gigantic investors such as Long-Term Capital Management and the firm's Nobel laureate managers. What became obvious to me as I wrote the book was that anticipating and responding to booms and busts required a committee of experts with a range of expertise. No single, siloed expert could make sense of why local and global economics hit uncertainty and then went over various cliffs.

There was, however, one major way in which the book differed from the course. I was determined to make the book "useful" to my readers and wanted to demonstrate the power of the *Boombustology* framework with a real-time case. I added a final chapter on China and its then-booming economy. My argument was that it couldn't last and might not even be as real as some of its advocates wished to claim.

It was a risky move to suggest that China was unstable or ahead of itself. Bill knew my views were iconoclastic and felt they deserved a public airing. My conclusion was that China's unprecedentedly fast, decades-long economic growth was less sustainable than people at that time believed. I argued that the *Boombustology* seismograph was registering an elevated risk of forthcoming chaos. I suggested that a credit-fueled investment bubble had grown too rapidly for too long. A slowdown was almost certain. In 2010, when I was writing the book, this was a blasphemous view in the world of finance and investing. By 2011, when the book came out, it was perhaps even more controversial. Western countries were still in the clutches of a global financial crisis, the effects of which had been, most experts declared, mitigated by China's stimulus and its impact on the world economy. At that moment, China was considered the world's savior. Everyone told me that the world economy was working only because China was working and that the only reason we all hadn't gone off the global financial cliff was courtesy of the People's Republic.

My multi-lens framework suggested that the Chinese economic story was more mirage than miracle. The dynamics of credit within the country had debt rising at alarming rates. And the signs of exuberance were everywhere. I remember hearing about the world's most expensive dog being purchased for millions by a Chinese entrepreneur. Sotheby's and Christie's were hiring native Mandarin speakers as quickly as they could find them. Real estate markets were so hot that the government had to limit the number of units individuals could buy. And yet, one analyst found that sixty million electricity meters were registering zero usage. It felt like a house of cards. And even the world's tallest skyscraper, a trusty indicator of forthcoming financial and economic chaos, was pointing to trouble as the Chinese launched multiple projects that sought to take the title from Dubai.

All the while, the global investment community marveled at how bureaucrats in Beijing were able to direct an economy more efficiently than markets. This last point stupefied me, as I thought the lesson of the Soviet Union's economic collapse was that centrally planned resource allocation was simply unable to keep up with the invisible hand directed by market prices.

And yet, to my surprise, my willingness to contradict the prevailing narrative also gave the book traction when I started to share my thesis publicly. I started speaking about my ideas on Bloomberg Radio, then a little bit on Bloomberg Television and CNBC, and then I published pieces in places such as *Forbes* and *Fortune*. Perhaps naively, I wanted to share my generalist framework for thinking about bubbles with the broadest possible audience. Instead, the world looked at me as an expert and wanted answers. What does this mean for commodity markets? Should we exit our Australian mining stocks? What does this mean for currency markets, the US dollar, US Treasury bonds, or even gold? Ironically, many of those who learned about my thinking from the book or my many media appearances sought my counsel because they viewed me as an expert, a specialist, even if I was demonstrating the power of generalist thinking. It was awkward to navigate the disconnect. I kept thinking, *The only thing I'm expert at is being a generalist. I'm an expert generalist.*

Various media gave me opportunities to explain why and how multi-lens thinking allows a person to spot the warning signs of booms and busts over the centuries. I'd observed that this approach worked not just on historical busts but also on contemporary booms, even not-yet-visible booms heading toward busts. Whether termed multi-lens thinking, or system thinking, or keeping experts on tap rather than on top, it all boiled down to behaving like a generalist, or as someone who drew on lots of resources to think for himself. In fact, it was the generalist logic that led to the analysis that was so different from the prevailing wisdom of China as an emerging super-economy that the investment community had coalesced around. Again and again, this was met with wise nods of heads; then a question inevitably followed: "But as an expert on booms and busts, what do you advise our listeners do with their retirement funds?"

"Think differently. Think generally," I would reply. "And then, think for yourselves." Curiously, though these answers were not what was wanted—my sense was they hoped for a more refined Jim Cramer of *Mad Money*, someone who would say (if not bark), "Buy!" or "Sell!"—the media kept constantly asking for my thoughts, perhaps because of this hope.

The publicity started to snowball in late 2011, leading to speaking engagements. I'll never forget the first invitation: it was for a conference of hedge-fund managers that was being held in Monaco. Would I like to come? To Monaco? Flights and accommodations covered? Well, sure! To make this pleasant surprise even better, I was able to bring Kristen along and stay in an oceanfront villa for three days. There, someone who heard my talk invited me to Stockholm to share my views with the country's sovereign funds as well as government officials. Not only did they pay my expenses, but they also provided an honorarium for my speech. I couldn't believe it. I was getting to fly first class to a great city, where I got to eat nice meals and talk with interesting people about a topic I was passionate about. And I was getting paid to do so!

The success of the book and the invitations to speak showed me the power of sidestepping the media and sharing ideas directly with the public. It also introduced me to the value, both in ideas and in dollars and cents, that the average person put on a generalist able to explain expertise. Sure, the world was filled with specialists, but that didn't mean there wasn't an embedded hunger for generalist thinking. There were plenty of dots. What many in the audiences I addressed seemed to crave was for someone to connect them in a coherent and meaningful way to produce new insights. While many had studied investor psychology or credit bubbles, few had connected the two (along with other dynamics) into an integrated framework. What I had done, in essence, was synthesize.

At this point, I had been working at SDK Capital, the spin-off hedge fund. I was helping to invest around $100 million of investor capital. The fund's principal was very generous and offered disproportionate compensation to anyone at the firm who might attract new business. Thus, any new business I could bring in would increase my take-home pay. Unsurprisingly, I would therefore routinely call foundations, sovereign wealth funds, and other allocators of capital to pitch the fund's investing services. At that point, our performance was quite good. The fund had, in fact, accomplished the rare feat of not losing money during the 2008 financial crash. Nevertheless, many institutions would never return my calls.

One of the people I couldn't get a meeting with was the chief investment officer of one of the largest foundations in the United States and a major investor in hedge funds. I had personally called his office several times and would never get a return call. One day, not long after the book was published, I returned to the office after doing a program on my book for Bloomberg Television to see a message from this man's office. But it wasn't to discuss business for the hedge fund—instead, it was asking me if I would come to the foundation to speak to its staff. There was no acknowledgment that I had been knocking on his door for years. As far as I knew, he was unaware of the irony. After all, he had dozens or more experts hoping to get minutes of his time. I had gone from being one of them to being an author with generalized insights into the behavior of markets and people. That I knew I was both-and, both expert and generalist, mattered less than this investor's desire for a generalist.

This sort of thing happened more than once during the year the book came out, and it got me thinking about the usefulness of my staying at the fund. There, I was confined to my supposed specialty and expected to apply a prescribed approach to my analysis. The success of *Boombustology* showed me there was an audience for my generalist approach and a wide world of subjects and ideas I could research and speak to. Charley's tragedy was morphing into triumph.

The questions to answer were, simply: Was I willing to put my own ideas into practice and think for myself (risking my salary and position to do so)? Was I willing to become a professional generalist, in fact? With Kristen's support, I took the leap, left SDK, and gave myself over to public speaking and public writing.

CHAPTER 23

A Professional Thinker

After a few months, the speaking invitations were flowing rapidly, and I simply couldn't keep up. I was overwhelmed and realized I needed help to manage my budding career as a public thinker. Through a fortuitous introduction, I had the opportunity to meet Tony D'Amelio, who had just launched a speaker management business. He was kind enough to take me on as a client. Tony had previously run the Washington Speakers Bureau's New York office, where he had worked with luminaries such as Ronald Reagan, Margaret Thatcher, and Colin Powell. He continued to represent big hitters like journalist Bob Woodward and NBA legend Bill Walton. I was beyond flattered that he decided to take on a virtually unknown first-time author, and with his help, I was able to get my ideas to audiences I'd never imagined speaking to—from corporate boardrooms to multiple-ballroom Vegas audiences.

This tour as a published author was a far cry from some prior experiences I'd had speaking in front of an audience as a specialist scholar. I'll never forget the time I was invited to an academic conference in Lausanne, Switzerland, around 2005 as a PhD student, and asked to speak at the end of the day. As evening approached, I noticed the crowd in the auditorium had started to thin out, so by the time it was my turn, there was one person left to hear what I had to say. *Well, this is stupid,* I thought. *Why should I waste our time giving a formal speech with this audience member when I can just talk to him directly?* So I approached this person, who was clearly a fan of my work—after all, why would he stick around to listen to me after everyone else had left?

"Hey there," I said, "why don't we go out, and I'll share my research with you over a cup of coffee?"

And that's when the guy said to me, "You don't understand, Vikram—I'm up next!"

I wrapped up quickly and left him to fill the auditorium as best he could.

Part of the genius of Tony D'Amelio is appreciating just how important it is to put the right ideas before the right audiences. Whereas the organizers of an academic conference filled time slots—who's talking at 6:00 p.m. in Ballroom B?—Tony understood what was possible when the staff at corporate boardrooms or conference organizers were eager to gain applicable insights from an outside speaker. Under Tony's direction, I was also able to broaden the subjects of my talks beyond the financial topics I'd written about in *Boombustology* to include some of my other interests.

One particular topic that seemed to resonate was that of the emergence of a global middle class and its implications for food supplies and food prices. It led to dozens of bookings with large audiences both inside and outside the agricultural industry. I also began talking about technology and its implications for energy, mining, and other global industries. Within years, I had speaking and consulting clients in the aerospace, mining, technology, agriculture, financial services, education, health care, construction, energy, and automotive sectors.

Thanks in large part to Tony, I've now addressed audiences on every continent outside of Antarctica. (I'm still hoping to book a room at the McMurdo Station someday!) He helped me grow my business and became a real partner and collaborator. To this day, I remain grateful for his encouragement, support, and invaluable guidance.

He also taught me a vital lesson about the generalist's profession: many businesses valued the generalist, even if they struggled to say so. Tony's network of speakers was built around pairing the right person to address the right subject before the right audience. Almost always, the audience, by way of their employer, knew the subject that needed to be addressed. They would seek out someone to speak to peak performance or the economy or health care or international politics. And Tony would respond, "I've got just the person!" He did, even if that individual was often someone who could speak to some, perhaps even all, of these subjects. What Tony's network taught me was that even if the world defaulted to speaking of experts and specialty subjects, in practice, it welcomed generalists who could say cogent, original, and practical things about a given subject. There was an under-the-surface but very real interest in the proverbial "big picture" and how challenges crossed the silos of traditional expertise.

Over time, this became an invitation to widen my range of interests by broadening my curiosity through research and seeking out opportunities to present these ideas to attentive listeners. This was a place where a professional generalist could thrive.

An anticipated quirk of being a professional generalist who was employed to travel broadly, speak on numerous subjects before diverse audiences, and work consistently to connect dots in ways meaningful to them was that I became a one-person firm. With help from Tony, of course, initially, I did it all. But only eventually did I add the trappings of typical employment, such as an office to drive to and an assistant to help with scheduling and client relations. As the world would come to appreciate during the COVID pandemic, working from home meant being both much more present and, if you weren't focused, much less productive.

Kristen was a wonder. She managed all aspects of Torit Montessori, which also extended to overseeing Tori's early education and encompassed the even earlier education of Kai, four years Tori's junior. I was around more but also sometimes more distracted. First with discipline, and only later with office space, an assistant, and a couple of analysts, was I able to balance the blurred lines of father and husband with being an entrepreneurial professional generalist.

The effort to keep these two worlds distinct was a challenge. More than anything, attempting to do so drove home the insight of Kristen's unique wisdom: she had made caring for children, starting with our own, her profession. Until I could manage a similar trick, I was left to juggle the responsibilities—and their diverse demands—as best I could.

CHAPTER 24

AN INDIAN AMONG COWBOYS

If there's one thing I learned from those exciting years after the publication of *Boombustology*, it is that when you open yourself up to it, the world is a weirder, wilder place than you can ever imagine. In a reenactment of the adventuresome spirit of the migrant mindset, I was learning that if a traveling generalist wants to get the most out of life, he should make himself available to the opportunities that come his way. Even if one of those opportunities ends up with you on the back of a horse you can barely ride, attempting to do rodeo tricks.

In late 2011, I was helping researchers at the Federal Reserve think about land bubbles. It so happened that while doing so, I received an invitation to talk about *Boombustology* with the CFA Society of Nebraska and Mutual of Omaha on the same trip. Having never been to the American heartland, I was immediately intrigued. I also felt it would help me understand more about the agriculture industry and learn a bit about a budding analytical interest of mine—the global food complex and, specifically, the cattle industry.

I had been studying global economic trends about what middle-class consumers do when they get more dispensable income, and one of the most consistent things they do is change their diets.

They start eating more meat. During the early twenty-first century, the world was witnessing a profound rise in the number of global middle-income households. I was interested in the economic, climate, and agricultural impact this change would have. I turned to some of the folks I knew at the Federal Reserve bank, and one of them suggested I reach out to Jim Timmerman: "He runs a feed yard not far from Omaha, and he was chair of the Omaha Branch of the Kansas City Fed. He's a super-nice guy and will probably be able to show you around a bit." I called Jim and arranged to meet up with him during my trip. He said he'd bring along his brother and business partner, Gerald.

The Timmermans leave an impression. The brothers were no-nonsense, no-bullshit, honest, hardworking Americans. They were courteous, frank, and dedicated. And they'd been able to successfully grow their cattle business upstream from feed yards into ranching and downstream into "harvesting" or "processing" (I learned those were the proper terms when I mistakenly referred to the processing facility as a "slaughterhouse"). Jim joined the US Army Infantry during the Vietnam era and was a member of the Reserves, in part out of a desire to give back to America, to contribute what he could. Gerald still treats a handshake like a contract.

One thing that really sticks out about my meeting the Timmermans was that despite their success, Jim and Gerald ran their business out of a small, nondescript, single-story office in Springfield, Nebraska. It was the opposite of corporate. During our first meeting in the conference room, in fact, a neighbor stopped by to ask about the location of a garden hose. No fancy pretenses here.

After talking business for a while, Jim and I both discovered that we loved Las Vegas. We became friends, and he later invited me and Kristen out to the National Finals Rodeo (NFR), which is held in Las Vegas every year. Thus began an annual tradition for me and Kristen—and the gradual countrification of my wardrobe! The first year, I showed up in jeans, a button-down shirt, and some casual shoes. I was given a pass, a Yankee interloper. The next year,

The Making of a Generalist

Kristen decided we were going to try to fit in, so we picked up a couple of "cowboy hats" at the Kittery Trading Post (KTP) in southern Maine. Upon arrival at the rodeo in Vegas, Gerald took one look at my knockoff hat and shook his head. "Your wife buy that at a five-and-dime? Throw it away!" I knew enough not to defend KTP as an institution that had been outfitting New Englanders for the outdoors, whether to hunt deer or climb Mount Washington, for nearly a hundred years. Rather, I followed the instructions of the local expert, and Gerald made sure I was outfitted with an authentic Stetson.

The next year, it was boots. I'd bought a shiny pair of cowboy boots before my first trip to Springfield and pulled them out of the closet for this trip. Upon arrival, they were deemed okay for plane travel by Gerald but not suitable for rodeo attendance. Gerald sorted me out again with an authentic pair. The year after that, it was time to address my jeans. "There are only two brands of jeans," I was told, "Wrangler or Cinch. That's it. You can't wear anything else when you come out here." To make a long story short, I can now watch the rodeo in a real cowboy outfit, even if my wallet is meaningfully slimmer as a result. Arriving in the "West" as a guest and migrant, I took the guidance of the locals, those whose world I had entered. I also did my part, helping however and whenever I could, even if it was to provide entertainment as the misplaced coastal city slicker.

This outfit came in handy when I was invited by Gerald to attend an annual weeklong ride of businessmen/horse-riding enthusiasts in Montana. I'd never been on a serious ride before, and it had been decades since I'd sat on the back of a horse. "I'm not great on horses," I told Gerald. "I need you to know I'm not a cowboy."

Gerald didn't miss a beat. "We got plenty of cowboys, Vikram," he said with a sly grin. "We're looking for an Indian." Gerald, who is in his eighties, is not a malicious person, nor is he politically correct. What he knew above all else was me and my sense of humor.

So, I, too, didn't miss a beat. "You know, I'm not that kind of Indian."

"I know that," he replied. "But these dumb fucks on the ride won't know the difference!" We had a hearty laugh about it, but he was genuine in his invitation for me to join him in his world.

In his own inimitable way, Gerald was putting me at ease. Yeah, he was saying, you'll be asked to sit a horse. Yeah, any number of people there will be far more experienced with livestock and ranches than you are. But, and this was the point, he and they wouldn't care. I was being invited to participate as no one other than myself.

Though I was a first-timer, I was included and felt immediately like I belonged. Also, as near as I could tell, no one was at all confused about what sort of "Indian" I was. What they figured out in a heartbeat, however, was that I was an American who knew precious little about sitting on a horse. The flavor of the event was one of genuine, pure, community-oriented camaraderie. Everyone pitched in, from serving and clearing tables to patching the occasional banged knee, a task left to the doctors among the attendees. There was even a gymkhana, which is a kind of mini-rodeo where riders compete in activities like barrel racing, pole bending, and other tests of horsemanship. My migrant mindset was on full display among these cowboys. I remain grateful to Lee Patterson, a true cowboy straight out of central casting, for his gracious instruction and patience in teaching me enough horsemanship over a couple of hours that I was able to avoid a hospital trip during my first rodeo.

One person deserves special mention for making me feel particularly welcome during the gymkhana: Michael Gallagher. He became a friend, a mentor, and someone who exhibited the kindness and understanding only possible from a life that had seen everything. You see, Mike had been a professional baseball player, a lawyer who argued before the US Supreme Court, and a titan in the corporate world—not to mention a dedicated family man and patriotic American.

He began by sharing stories of prior riders: "One guy punctured a lung, broke a few ribs, and had to be rushed to the hospital. We've had dislocated shoulders and many other issues." After I was sufficiently nervous, the softer side of Mike emerged: "You'll be fine. Get on the horse and ride; it knows what to do. If you fall off, it's user error. Good luck!" I realized that Mike was acting as a good host, and in turn, I was a willing good guest.

I'm pleased to report that I survived my first rodeo. In the end, Mike's advice proved invaluable. I relied on the horse's expertise, and it served me well. Even better, I can now say, without hesitation and with the conviction that accompanies truth, "This is not my first rodeo."

CHAPTER 25

DOES BREADTH TRUMP DEPTH?

The publication of *Boombustology* opened the door to numerous opportunities, like joining a group of actual cowboys for a ride, while introducing me to the profession of being a generalist. Others use the shorthand of "public intellectual," "influencer," and even "devil's advocate." None of these fits nearly as well as "professional generalist." I had earned a PhD in innovation to give rigor and method to my childhood inheritance of a migrant mindset, both-and thinking, and exercising adaptation within uncertainty. The more I explored its possibilities, the more I came to understand that a generalist approach wasn't anything new, except for how it was applied, the sort of research it entailed, and the professional habits of detailed curiosity it instilled. The more and wider I read, the more I realized that American history was filled with generalists. Benjamin Franklin, Abigail Adams, Thomas Edison, Dwight Eisenhower, Eleanor Roosevelt, Ronald Reagan: across all industries and areas of endeavor, I found them, taking increasing encouragement that it was a profession I, too, could follow.

What the lives of these professional generalists taught was that their accomplishments were less determined by their expertise than by their interests, methods, and curiosity. Franklin was America's original polymath, Adams had a genius for real estate and (as a wife to and mother of presidents) politics, Edison was a corporate entrepreneur, and Eisenhower helped win WWII and position America to eventually win the Cold War. These were generalists of extraordinary and enviable influence.

Growing up, Ronald Reagan was one of my heroes. During the two terms of his presidency, I found that my awareness of politics and policies increased marginally, year over year, but my immediate reaction to the man was apolitical. He seemed so normal, so able to articulate common sense that seemed so noncontroversial to me. To this day, I remember his 1984 presidential ad about "Morning in America," in which Americans were heading back to work, inflation was falling, and people were buying homes. Only ten at the time, I distinctly remember asking my parents how an actor could become president of the United States. Without missing a beat, they replied, in a very Reaganesque manner: because this is America. He embodied the very American Dream that he sought to protect and did so with a devout belief in limited government, something that especially resonated with my parents.

I took from all these historical examples of successful generalists the ever-firmer conviction that I would be a full-time, professional generalist. That's how I would make my own contributions to the world.

After four years of teaching my course on booms and busts, I planned and began teaching a new class on business ethics, which I initially co-taught with Charley. Our approach to the subject was not prescriptive. We took as a given that a professor can't instill a sense of ethics in college students, nor is it possible to create a list of rules that can cover every ethical conundrum a future business leader might confront. Therefore, we saw it as our mission to expose students to the ethical complexities businesses encounter and to discuss the various choices leaders could make when faced with them.

Adventures in Business Ethics, as the class was titled, was very popular with students, but because it was a small seminar, there wasn't room to accept everyone who wanted to take the class. Demand far exceeded capacity. One year, I had accepted fifteen students who were seniors in the department, who were writing their senior essays about business ethics, or who'd been denied access to other senior seminars. That left ten seats for students who showed up to the first class. So when fifty students showed up for those ten remaining seats, the class was immediately faced with its own ethical dilemma: What is the fairest way to decide who gets into the class?

"This may just seem like logistics," I told them, "but it's the essence of ethics—making tough choices. First lesson—let's figure out the students who will be in the class."

One of the students, a senior in the department, put on his coat to leave. I asked if he was dropping the class. "Nope," he said. "I'm getting breakfast. I was already 'in' the class through the preselection process. I don't need to waste my time with this." True, as a senior in the department, he was listed as accepted into the class. Not true, however, was that this meant his enrollment was a given. He exited, and I struck his name off the list of enrolled students that I had scribbled on the board—why waste any *more* of *his* time? Surely, a willingness to attend class should be a basic criterion. Now there were eleven seats available for the fifty students who wanted in. But that still meant thirty-nine wouldn't be accommodated. And I decided on the spot that the criteria for those offered seats would be determined completely by the entire group of people competing for them. What did they think the guiding principle should be?

You may not be shocked to hear that their arguments were all a bit self-serving. "The class should have a diversity of majors," noted an art major. "I think it's critical that seniors get priority," said a senior. An Australian student thought it was very important that the class have a foreign perspective. One student who had tried to get into the class last year suggested, "Those who have tried in prior years should be given preference." Much to my amusement, one student from a country with suspicions of mass corruption suggested, "Those from countries lacking rule of law would be able to benefit most from the class."

None of these were bad arguments, but how to choose among them? I let the class continue debating. Finally, they arrived at a system that prioritized seniority but included a healthy dose of randomness. They discovered that sometimes it was impossible to develop rules that would satisfy everyone's idea of fairness, no matter how well intentioned. And they left that first class with a deeper understanding that business ethics, like economics more generally, is a world of trade-offs and ambiguities, most fairly dealt with when made transparent. What they learned was that strict adherence to any individual's "expert" vantage point—be it that of an Australian or an art student—guaranteed a sense of unfairness; they also came to respect that a focus on process over outcomes might lead to improved legitimacy of the results.

As a person guided by a generalist mindset, I love the challenges posed by ethical dilemmas, especially in business. The latter because it involves so many competing perspectives and obligations. In conversation with Charley, we felt it was one of our missions to challenge these students' assumptions and their tendency for groupthink, which is pervasive on college campuses and in offices. What a serious exploration of ethical quandaries can expose is that a lot of the beliefs humans hold dear, often under the guise of their expert understanding of the issue, don't stand up to scrutiny because they haven't properly challenged those beliefs.

To bring each subject to life, I brought in guests from the business world to talk about the very real, complicated issues they faced when running their companies. These guests were designed to challenge and provoke the students. For example, I asked students to think about the thorny issue of assigning a monetary value to human life by inviting Ken Feinberg, a world-renowned expert on victim compensation, to speak about his work to the class. Alex Epstein, author of *The Moral Case for Fossil Fuels*, challenged the conventional analysis that informs a lot of environmental policy and compelled students to think about the importance of prioritizing humans in designing energy policy. I even asked Noel Biderman, the founder, chairman, and CEO of Ashley Madison, the online dating service designed to facilitate extramarital affairs, to discuss whether it was wrong for the company to profit from adultery.

The students' reactions were always the best part for me. During the Ashley Madison case, for example, one of the students stood up, walked around the conference room table, and stood towering over Noel. As I worried about physical violence and imagined headlines of "Mansharamani fired after class degenerates into fistfight," the student began a passionate argument.

"You! You're breaking up families! My father cheated on my mother, and it broke up our family. My sister still won't trust men. You're encouraging this behavior!"

After the student sat down, Noel respectfully responded, "I'm sorry to hear about that . . . but your story confirms what we all know—namely, that adultery has been going on for thousands of years. What Ashley Madison is doing is taking it out of the workplace, which will make businesses more efficient, and making it discreet, which means more couples will stay together, which we know is good for kids—kids in single-parent households do less well in life. So, I'm actually helping society more than you realize."

My students then discussed whether they agreed with Noel, whether they'd invest in his business, and whether any of them would accept a job working with him. He did offer extraordinary compensation and invited anyone in the class who was interested to reach out. As far as I know, no one did.

The effectiveness of this approach was clear from the students' reactions. I was also becoming a confident professional generalist. No, I wasn't accomplishing things like my professional generalist heroes from across American history. But I was well employed, creating and sharing ideas drawn from across disciplines and domains that diverse audiences heard and applied with appreciation. A rising number of corporations and organizations paid me to speak with their staff, sit on their boards, and offer them management advice. There were always more Yale undergraduates eager to take my classes than there were available seats. I had an office to drive to and a minimal staff to help run my professional generalist business. Life seemed, at least then, to be "on track."

And then I got a nudge to consider whether there was an opportunity to think differently about what I was saying and where my thinking might prove helpful.

CHAPTER 26

FOXY THINKING

An older gentleman who had heard me speak about *Boombustology* was making diligent efforts to track me down. I'm embarrassed to say that I didn't avoid him so much as I failed to prioritize him. There was much going on in the office, there were papers to grade, and there was my cherished home life that I always wished to give more time to. So when someone I couldn't place contacted me via Yale, it took me a while to eventually call him back.

"I want to thank you," he began. "Your talk helped my wife and me navigate a cancer diagnosis."

I had a flashback to my friends making fun of the Dr. Mansharamani title, and I initially assumed this kind person had tracked down the wrong Mansharamani.

"I'm sorry, sir—I think you have the wrong person."

He was adamant and recalled with clarity a conversation he and I had had after I'd given a talk. As he did so, I called to memory his face and our conversation. "Ah, yes, I do remember," I allowed. Then I added, "We were speaking of financial bubbles. I am quite sure I never said anything about cancer."

He interrupted. "I know! But it wasn't financial bubbles you were teaching—at least not to me. When we spoke, we focused on the multi-lens approach you recommended. And I'm calling to tell you that I found it exceedingly helpful when my wife and I were making decisions regarding treatment. Or as we ended up choosing, the lack of treatment."

He had my attention. Even when addressing financial considerations, I always made clear that the generalist approach is an approach—a process, not an outcome. The promise is that it is a method by which you can apply the process, think for yourself, and reach an outcome. Outcomes matter, but the process of arriving at them matters more because that's how you can be confident that you have optimized thinking for yourself.

"You taught us to use multiple perspectives, and that gave us the confidence to make our own decisions," the man explained. "And as luck would have it, my wife is now in remission. Because we balanced experts and our own research and decisions, she avoided dealing with nausea and the other side effects from what, in her case, would have likely been unnecessary treatment." He paused, then said the thing that stuck with me: "You may think you were talking about finance, but you were talking about understanding uncertainty and making decisions in the face of it. Anyway, I just wanted to thank you."

I was blown away. For weeks thereafter, my rides to and from New Haven were dominated by my mulling over this kind man's insight. Since leaving Yale, I had mostly maintained a presumptive wall between navigating uncertainty as a profession and navigating uncertainty as a matter of being alive. My career, my degrees, my publications had all been focused on exploring and building out the former while allowing that uncertainty was no less present outside of work. I had just been slow to connect those particular dots. And having seen this, I was increasingly eager to connect them. When the Harvard Kennedy School offered me an opportunity to dig a bit deeper into an area of interest, I jumped at it.

Before I could join the Mossavar-Rahmani Center for Business and Government as a senior fellow, its leadership wanted me to spell out just what I intended to make the focus of my research. I submitted a program of research around the following questions: Does a generalist navigate complex decisions in the face of overwhelming uncertainty better than someone who focuses narrowly? In more simple terms, in times of confusion—and no matter the cause of the confusion or where you encounter it—does breadth trump depth?

I was invited to begin in September 2013, which gave me some runway to develop these questions into a more formal research plan. And in the fine tradition of a multitasking generalist, I based the research agenda for my Kennedy School fellowship on a TED talk I had given at Yale in 2012.

In February 2012, I appeared on stage at a TED event at Yale University to present "The Power of Foxy Thinking." The title was a reference to the ancient Greek parable about the hedgehog that knows one big thing and the fox that knows many things. It was also an early articulation of some of the themes relating to the importance of a generalist mindset that I write about in this book, about how it's possible to outfox uncertainty. But when I recall that TED talk today, I don't think much about what I said or how well it was received. All that comes to mind is how heavy, tired, and out of shape I was at that time, caught permanently in that video. Though I was still playing squash regularly, I was about fifty-five pounds over my college weight and maybe thirty more than I was just a few years before.

This was more than just the expanding waistline most of us experience as we hit middle age, and Kristen and I had different theories about what was going on. I had only recently left the hedge fund, with all its demands of travel, long hours, and lost sleep. She believed that I was experiencing the accumulated effects of years of stress and tiredness from that job (and perhaps maybe a few too many rich meals). I, on the other hand, wondered if there was something wrong with my metabolism. There had been no obvious changes in what I ate, and I was exercising about as much as I always had. There must be a cause, I reasoned, but what was it?

At this point, I was sleeping two to three hours in the afternoon each day, which was not sustainable. So I went to my general practitioner (GP), who ran me through a prescribed gauntlet of examinations for these symptoms. But after weeks of tests for Lyme disease, viruses, mononucleosis, and other ailments, my GP could find nothing wrong with me. "Why don't we send you to a specialist?" my GP suggested. My alarm bells immediately went off. I had, of course, recently written a book suggesting that financial specialists were potentially less likely to see financial bubbles than were those who looked through multiple lenses. And I had begun to sense a similar logic in other domains, driven in large part by a book titled *Expert Political Judgment* written by Philip Tetlock that suggested a similar dynamic in political forecasting. (It would be another year before I had my conversation with the man who had followed the process laid out in *Boombustology* to a better treatment plan for his wife.)

Regardless, when my doctor suggested I see a specialist, I was suspicious. I was teaching a course about how specialists spend so much time studying bark that they can't see the trees, let alone the forest. Was turning to a specialist really the best approach to what seemed to be a complex, holistic problem?

I asked the doctor, "If you're sending me to a specialist, what kind of specialist, and why?" The doctor told me my liver enzyme levels were slightly high, so he suggested I see a hepatologist. And that was where I jumped off the train of modern medicine. I would have had no problem seeing a liver specialist if I'd had an acute issue, but I was not about to have a person who is focused intensely on one organ of the body start making medical decisions about my vague, chronic issue. I was facing uncertainty, and my gut told me a specialist was not the right approach. I listened to myself.

I wanted to get to the bottom of the mystery but simply couldn't shake my skepticism. Thus began some personal field research into the different medical philosophies that inform the treatment of complex biological problems. What could I learn about different ways medicine is practiced, and what should we all be wary of?

As I read about different medical approaches, I was immediately drawn to Eastern medicine, which is much more holistic than Western medicine. Yet, it was difficult to find rigorous scientific research about it. So I kept digging and soon came across a field known as functional medicine, a systems biology–based approach that focuses on identifying and addressing the root cause of an issue. Upon encountering it, I had an immediate sense of recognition and philosophical alignment. It was a holistic approach to health that was in many ways the opposite of the specialist pyramid around which much of our health-care system has been built.

Traditional primary care physicians begin with symptoms. Functional doctors start with how the body is functioning, an approach based on a deep conviction that most symptoms are manifestations of bodily malfunctions. Whereas traditional doctors seek to make symptoms disappear, often with pharmaceuticals or other treatments, functional doctors focus on tackling the root cause of the malfunction. The fact that functional doctors are board-certified MDs gave me confidence that there was a scientific basis for their approach.

As a dyed-in-the-wool generalist, I was sold. The next step was to find a functional doctor to treat me. I reached out to the chairman of the Institute for Functional Medicine, Dr. Mark Hyman of the UltraWellness Center. After a short time on his waiting list, I made the trek to Lenox, Massachusetts, to see him. Almost immediately after we exchanged pleasantries, Mark took out a pen and began scribbling on a notepad. "All right, Vikram, I've got some tests I want to recommend."

"But, Doctor," I said, "you don't even know why I'm here!"

To which he replied, "Vikram, *you* don't know why you're here."

And he was right. Touché. Then he explained that functional medicine required him to painstakingly isolate all the potential causes of my fatigue.

"The way this functional field works," he went on, "I've got to figure out whether you have vitamin deficiencies. I've got to check your hormone levels. I need to understand any toxic elements in your body and allergies you may have. Symptoms have many causes. So let's start by gathering some information about what's going on in your body. Sound good?"

I was treated to another battery of tests, which went well beyond the ones my GP had administered. It wasn't cheap, and much of it wasn't covered by insurance, but I was interested in where it was going. Not only because Dr. Hyman's approach jibed with my own outlook on problem-solving but also because I secretly hoped that I could learn something from this experience that might help with Tori and give us insights into approaches that would be positive and constructive for her. Maybe she had complicating issues that hadn't been addressed. Or conversely, maybe there were treatments for some of the contributing factors that hadn't been identified. If such insights were a result, I was happy to be a guinea pig.

Thanks to the wide battery of tests that considered my body's unique chemistry, we learned that I had high levels of mercury and aluminum, a vitamin D deficiency, and celiac disease. I was able to address these imbalances by changing my diet; using different and more natural deodorants, soaps, and shampoos; and taking supplements. And six months later, I began to feel a lot better and started losing weight. In the end, I dropped about sixty pounds over eighteen months. Indeed, I got to the point where I was feeling so much better that I set a goal to run the Boston Marathon, which I'm pleased to share that I did (as a charity runner) in 2017!

CHAPTER 27

EXPERT AFTER EXPERT

Since I was no longer working at the hedge fund, I'd been spending more time at home with the kids. Kai was running around our apartment like a typical toddler and growing quickly. I'd missed a lot due to my long work hours, so it was a joy to catch up on some of those lost moments. Watching Tori and Kai interacting was a delight. Tori was a proud sister, super excited about her brother. She was protective, caring, and doting; the relationship was special and brought me to tears on multiple occasions. And Kai was emerging as a wonderful little brother, respectful and supportive of his older sister.

Spending a lot of time with Tori also made me more aware of her developmental issues. To address them, Kristen and I had sought the advice of professionals to find the best ways to meet her needs, and we encountered an utter lack of consensus. Developmental psychologists said one thing, her teacher thought something else, and her pediatrician believed something else entirely. Tori, of course, had opinions of her own, and contemplating the best ways forward for our child routinely put Kristen and me in painful, loving uncertainty.

I had approached functional medicine with my own medical concerns in mind. But just as most parents would have done, I always had one eye out for what might help my kids. This was especially true when it came to Tori; anything that might provide an insight or offer a benefit, I was willing to explore.

As I began to see the success I was having with the approach Dr. Hyman coordinated to address my problems with weight gain and fatigue, Kristen and I agreed to investigate whether the method could help Tori, too. So began one of the more difficult, painful, and self-enlightening years of my life.

In retrospect, I can see that my positive experience with functional medicine gave me unreasonable expectations and an unfair comparison. I had sought out functional medicine knowing that I needed to gain energy, lose weight, and get better sleep. I was willing to experiment with different means and different processes toward that hoped-for outcome. It was one thing for me to submit myself to a battery of tests and needle pokes, but it was heartbreaking to compel Tori to do so. For starters, she didn't even understand what, if anything, was "wrong." How do you explain to a kid that she needs to fast or can't have a birthday cake because she might have a sensitivity to gluten? We also gave her vitamins and supplements, but it was impossible to register much change from these treatments. This, Kristen and I concluded, reflected that she was only six years old, and tracking subjective improvements was therefore difficult.

Eventually, however, we decided that functional medicine would not provide the same insights and benefits to her as it had for me. Unfortunately, this also meant we were back to the world of specialists. We were living in Brookline at the time, which arguably has one of the better school districts in the state. But under the specialists' battery of experts and educational programs, Tori still struggled. Seeking answers, we took her to Boston Children's Hospital, arguably one of the best facilities in the world. Frustratingly, the hospital's collection of experts didn't know what to make of Tori, either. One of them would opine that their field of expertise held the key to addressing her problems, only to conclude, days or weeks or months later, that nope, they couldn't figure out what was wrong, either. And so it went for months. All of this put Kristen and me through cycles of manic energy—"I think they've figured it out!"—followed by depression: "We've learned nothing and tortured Tori."

Finally, we got the name of a supposedly cutting-edge neurologist who was interested in Tori's case. He suggested more tests to examine her genetics and map her brain. We were initially reluctant to expose Tori, once again, to a scary series of tests, but we ultimately relented. After all, perhaps this would be the grail we'd been seeking. I still vividly remember one of the saddest moments in my life, sitting with Tori in the waiting room to go in for a brain scan, with her asking us, "Why am I here? Is everything okay?"

To Tori's tremendous credit, she was trusting and, for the most part, willing to try. Exactly what her parents were trying to figure out wasn't clear to her, but she was willing to believe that they had her best interests at heart. The tests continued. At one point, shortly after one such test, the doctor called us. "Hey, the results are in, and we're going to get on the phone to discuss them, but we need to have a counselor on the phone also."

Then he made it clear that it would be another forty-eight hours before the counselor would be available and the call could be scheduled. We spent those two days in a panic, reading up on every genetic disorder you could imagine. We were petrified. Finally, the time for the dreaded call arrived. Kristen and I sat together, looking at our phone set to speaker. And with the counselor present, the doctor said, "Yeah. Listen, we've done all the brain scans, and there doesn't appear to be any anomalies." It was hospital policy not to reveal genetic tests without a counselor on the phone.

At first, there was a sense of profound relief. But about an hour later, I was as angry as I've ever been in my life. It wasn't only for the two days of stress and anxiety the hospital had forced us to live through while waiting for a phone call that lasted only a few minutes. There was also the realization that we were back to square one. It took me longer than I wish to admit, but eventually, it did dawn on me. We were back to where we started. And maybe that wasn't such a bad place to be.

We'd tried everything we could think of to find answers to the problems that Tori had. Along the way, we came to understand that perhaps, just maybe, they were less problems than challenges. And more than anything, they were *Tori's* challenges. We'd spent years tapping the knowledge of expert after expert, and if you stepped back and assessed the results, none of them knew anything more insightful than any of the others. The conclusion was clear: Tori was Tori, and she would need to learn to think for herself, to navigate the world on her own terms. Our job was to help her do so as much as we could. She didn't need to be "fixed"—she needed to be supported within an environment that worked for her.

CHAPTER 28

YOUR LATEST?

As I explored how to think and act like a generalist at home, I discovered that doing so also informed my career as a professional generalist. What I recognized was that generalists do not get to rest on their laurels. Instead of a pinnacle achievement, a job title, or a particular award, generalists must remain in constant motion, always on a journey toward understanding today's and tomorrow's topics. You see, it is in motion, not at a destination, that generalists are most likely to spot opportunities. Once you start to think for yourself, you realize you have to keep doing so. It's a bit like a treadmill. The minute you stop being a broad, independent thinker—and commit to a fixed, specific viewpoint—you create a roadblock for generalist thinking. Conversely, the more you make independent thinking a deliberate practice, the more opportunities you'll encounter—with fewer full-stop challenges.

In the fall of 2014, I noticed that my speaking opportunities were declining. Three years had passed since the publication of *Boombustology*, and I had filled that time with consulting, teaching, and addressing audiences. But as the publication date of *Boombustology* receded further into the past, I was getting fewer invitations.

I wasn't the only one to notice. Tony D'Amelio was his usual forthright self. "Vikram," he told me, "if you want to keep your speaking business active and as vibrant as it's been for the last few years, you've got to give me fresh content. I need reasons to connect with the bureaus and remind them about you."

I was just naive enough to wonder why. After all, I had spent years earning degrees, gaining experience, working, and teaching about a range of topics. Not a week went by without my turning a curiosity into a multi-lens research interest that I then worked into a generalized insight. Take, for example, the connection between the world's tallest buildings and bubbles. Exercising wide-lens curiosity had introduced me to the fact that skyscrapers were one of the most robust indicators of a bubble. Consider the following: the financial panic of 1907 fell right as the Singer (187 meters) and Metropolitan Life (247 meters) Buildings were being completed in New York City; the Chrysler Building (329 meters) and the Empire State Building (443 meters) were completed at the start of the Great Depression; Petronas Towers (452 meters) in Kuala Lumpur was finished right when the Asian financial crisis hit; and in 2008–2009, as the world entered the global credit crunch, Dubai completed the Burj Dubai (828 meters).

Connecting those dots had everything to do with my interest in booms and busts, but Tony was telling me that for booking audiences, I needed to provide new material. What were my latest thoughts? "What about the fact that China is now constructing the world's tallest tower?" I quipped. He smiled and said, "Good, but I need a steady stream of your thinking, ideally in a form that I can send to bureaus." Perhaps another book? A newly published tome would be useful on many fronts, foremost of which would be that the media attention might reinvigorate my speaking business.

In the world of public speaking, there are three types of speakers: (1) celebrities who have been made famous by virtue of their experiences, the roles they've played, or the positions they've held; (2) inspirational speakers who can give a moving, sermon-like delivery that ignites an enthusiastic and visceral, emotional response and leads the audience to act; and (3) idea-oriented speakers who deliver compelling content in an engaging, thought-provoking manner. Sure, there are other types, but these categories serve to capture much of the world. I was clearly an "ideas" or "content" speaker, even though I might argue that I tried to inspire audiences to think differently. Regardless, in the eyes of speakers bureau agents and event organizers, my expertise was determined by the reception of my ideas, by my ability to engage an audience with not just facts but also a compelling delivery. At the root of it all, of course, were ideas. The implication seemed to be that if I wanted to keep making a living as a professional generalist, I needed to become a specialist at churning out ideas, content that was commonly and most traditionally delivered via books.

Unsurprisingly, this set me on a path to discover a better way.

Tony was, of course, right. Books have a half-life, and *Boombustology* had been out for a couple of years. To remain a relevant speaker means advancing new ideas and sustaining a conversation with a growing audience, and for decades, books had signaled that you were doing precisely that. Sure, I'd been writing the occasional *Forbes* or Bloomberg piece every few months or so, but I knew I needed to make a conscious effort to increase my output *and* my reach.

The particulars and practices of assessing widely diverse sources of information and translating that information in actionable and targeted ways, all while navigating uncertainty, were my professional bread and butter. My travel not only gave me insights, but it also gave me time—there is nothing like hours on an airplane to encourage productivity. I had no shortage of things to say and time to get my ideas down; what I needed was a way to put those ideas before readers.

So in late 2014, I set myself the task of writing a short piece every week for my personal website. It was a good exercise—and helpful to the speakers bureaus—but it didn't generate a lot of traffic. That's when I decided to start posting these pieces on LinkedIn. My thinking was simple: Why try to convince readers to come to my website when I could simply put my ideas where they were already spending time?

The difference in potential audiences was a compelling motivator. Instead of dozens of monthly visitors to my website, LinkedIn was receiving hundreds of millions. The bump in readership was immediate, even if not substantial. I recall that my first piece posted in January 2015 reached a few hundred visitors. And my audience grew with each week, with more and more readers sharing and engaging with my articles. There are several ways to track consequential ideas, including book sales, but LinkedIn was providing me with another. How many people were following, responding to, and sharing my posts? I soon found my articles reaching a thousand readers weekly; then it snowballed to 2,500 or so, then to 5,000, and eventually toward 10,000 or so regular readers of everything I wrote and posted.

Another thing I liked about LinkedIn was that I was my own gatekeeping editor. If I were pitching a piece to a magazine or news organization, they always asked me to narrow the range of my interests. Their expectations were that I would focus on a specific domain related to what I was teaching or writing about at the time. Mansharamani, the expert on bubbles, or asset prices, or innovation, or business ethics. I wanted to continue to share my thoughts on these subjects, but as a generalist, there was so much more I wanted to write about, and I liked connecting lots of disparate ideas in surprising ways—something institutional editors were not always comfortable with.

I was beginning to learn that just as there were discipline-specific scholars, they had their counterparts in discipline-specific editors. What seemed bizarre to me, then and now, was that scholars and editors both understood that readers weren't discipline specific. Sure, there were readers of business books and magazines, but they also bought and read biographies, novels, and articles on economics and local affairs. All these editors frequently declared their desire to reach what they themselves called "general readers." Yet, these same editors also wanted "experts" with "platforms" from which they were to be "on message." It seemed somewhere between counterproductive and inane—and a problem that online sites like LinkedIn solved by leaving authors in control.

LinkedIn gave me the freedom to write about a multiplicity of subjects: it might be fish farming one week, then the limitations of the Myers-Briggs test the next. My subsequent columns might jump into the latest news from China, discuss what was happening with lithium mining in Latin America, or address problems with grade inflation at American universities. On LinkedIn, I wasn't in a box, and I could apply my generalist perspective and different lenses to whatever was happening in the world at that moment. It was liberating, and I was getting a decent number of readers, though perhaps not the mythical "general audience" that book and magazine editors speak of. And then one day, one of my pieces went viral.

This was in February of 2015. Kristen, Tori, Kai, and I had visited Ogunquit, Maine, and at one point on the trip, I'd taken a great picture of lobster boats moving through some ocean ice floating in the harbor of Perkins Cove. A number of factors were then influencing New England lobstermen to prolong their season, which was a recent development. One such factor, I knew, was a surging demand in China for lobsters around the Chinese New Year. This was due to the Chinese growing wealthier—with more income to spend, they had developed an appetite for these tasty crustaceans. But there was something else, something that microeconomic trend watchers and supply-chain experts were likely to miss. In addition to being a luxury food, lobsters also happen to be red, which is an auspicious color in Chinese culture.

A microeconomic trend (China's rising middle class) and a quirk of psychology (the desire to demonstrate new wealth by purchasing luxuries) crossed with a sociological-cultural fact (red is considered auspicious) had come together to encourage Maine lobster boats to navigate sea ice.

It turned out that 2015 was the Chinese Year of the Sheep, so in the spirit of playfulness, I wrote an article connecting Maine's thriving lobster business with this unexpected driver of global lobster demand. The piece, titled "Sheep Pulling Lobsters from Snow," was read by tens of thousands of people—a significant improvement on my previous posts.

I was hooked. How far could I go? How many general readers could I reach?

By the end of the year, I had written approximately fifty-two articles about my travels to places like Vietnam, the suggestion that our quest for diversity was misguided, and even a tribute to baseball great Yogi Berra after he passed. These posts were arguably more influential and reached more people than many of my pieces for legacy media outlets. In fact, LinkedIn ran an algorithm to measure the influence of pieces posted on the site that factored in not only how many people read an article but also how frequently it was shared, how many likes it received, and how often recipients continued to share it. The results were grouped in various subject areas, and as it turned out, the number-one voice in the money and finance category was me. I was reaching hundreds and hundreds of thousands of readers. At the end of 2015, LinkedIn publicly honored me as its #1 Top Voice in Money & Finance.

CHAPTER 29

Escaping Refresh Mania

It might seem unusual, but I was never at a loss for topics. Having something to say wasn't the difficulty. I continued to undertake research for various clients and address audiences across the globe. Rarely was it dull, and sometimes it was heart racing. It was in Africa, en route to an airport, that I was advised by my "security" escort to keep my head down for fear of gunfire, which didn't prevent me from registering that they ran every red light rather than stopping the vehicle. It was in Colombia that I met with Frank Pearl, who at the time was leading peace negotiations between the Revolutionary Armed Forces of Colombia (FARC) rebels and the Colombian government. We even considered whether I should join him in Cuba to help paint a picture of shared regional prosperity to gain adherents to his peace plan. I was game, until it was pointed out that if I had any contact with the FARC, I would thereafter be tagged as having associated with a known terrorist group and imperil my ability to continue international travel. The stories I generated from my normal course of activities provided a steady stream of interesting material.

Tony used these results to help grow my speaking business, and I took them as inspiration to delve into even more eclectic and controversial topics. What I wasn't interested in was feeding people insights they already believed or wanted to hear. Under the old adage

"Give them what they want," this seems like an easy way to earn and maintain a readership. I just didn't buy that past preferences were predictive of future interests. I decided to treat my general readers as readers with general (and broad) interests.

After all, it had been a tenet of my life that people are more open to new ideas (e.g., a hands-free shower) and are more willing to consider them than is usually believed. The trick is to get the reader's attention with something provocative (e.g., "Look, Ma, no hands!") and then challenge them to think about the subject differently. And that is what I sought to do with my LinkedIn posts. I wanted people with opposing viewpoints to find something of value in what I wrote.

For the most part, I was able to successfully thread this needle. Indeed, I became ever more skilled at it, often setting my sights on ever more complicated efforts. Take, for example, a popular piece on Saudi Arabia I wrote in April of 2016, during the period when Mohammed bin Salman was rising to power with promises to modernize his country and transition its economy away from oil production. The piece acknowledged the challenges of a socially conservative nation like Saudi Arabia completely reimagining its economic system while at the same time not dismissing the possibility of it managing radical reform. I balanced these two perspectives consciously—I was curious if I could say something that both fans and critics of Saudi Arabia could agree on.

By then practiced in the art of social media headlines, I knew a thing or two about reader engagement. I gave the piece the title "Saudi Arabia on the Brink," a title ambiguous enough to speak to a wide potential audience. Some of my readers no doubt thought, *Yeah, Saudi Arabia is on the brink of total collapse!* Meanwhile, bullish readers no doubt concluded, *Yes! Saudi Arabia is finally shedding its medieval past and is on the brink of taking off!* The actual piece took a much more nuanced and less definitive position on the country's future, which was, in fact, what I hoped both sides of this debate would take away from reading it. The piece, which was picked up by other publications, reached well over one million readers and spurred engagement from members of the Saudi royal family, political and corporate leaders, and many journalists.

Because of the popularity of my pieces and my algorithmically determined identity as an influential person on the platform, the folks at LinkedIn began asking me to weigh in more on current events. And eager to raise my profile, I obliged. I will also admit I was flattered by the positive feedback I was getting in the form of "likes" and "follows" to my page. Until one day in November of 2016, when I had an epiphany about my increasingly troublesome relationship with online media.

My disenchantment with LinkedIn came about quite suddenly. I had published a piece on the site—I can no longer remember what it was about—and I realized that in the hour after I had clicked the "Post" button, I had refreshed the page more than twenty times. Like a day trader, I was frantically monitoring my shares. Click, refresh. Click, refresh. Click, refresh. I remember having this sensation of being outside myself, watching this zombie Vikram staring at the screen and repeatedly hitting a button like a chimpanzee in a behavioral science experiment. This ridiculous image briefly interrupted the dopamine feedback loop I was caught in and gave me a moment to think about how I was using LinkedIn and, more importantly, how it was using me. I thought about how I would occasionally, upon waking up in the middle of the night, grab my phone to check the latest numbers. It was compulsive—I just had to look.

With no small amount of irony, I worried that I was morphing into the very magazine editors I had sought to distance myself from. I was allowing audience metrics to guide my content decisions rather than allowing my curiosities and work to find new ways to think about challenges, the uncertainties that guide them, and how I could present these to readers to spark "think for yourself" moments. The very constraints I had liberated myself from by using LinkedIn were creeping in via a back door.

It was my valuing the ability to speak broadly and think generally that had attracted me to online media. If that very outlet was constraining my ability to do that, my experiment with it had run its course. Shortly after this eureka moment, I decided to limit my engagement with LinkedIn. And though I normally wouldn't recommend following the advice of *Seinfeld*'s George Costanza, on one thing he was undeniably correct: always end on a high note. Fortunately, my work in 2016 provided such an opportunity.

When the LinkedIn folks ran their annual influence algorithms on the millions of articles published on their platform during the year, they once again determined that I was their #1 Top Voice in the category of money, finance, and the global economy. And with an online membership network that had crossed a half-billion users at the time, this was an honor and recognition that caught the attention of many speakers bureaus. A perfect high note to end on. And so, when I finally posted my 2017 annual prediction piece—the most important developments I thought would happen in the years ahead—I quit writing my weekly piece.

Sure, I would write down my thoughts once a month or so, but I made a point of not monitoring the metrics as assiduously as I once had. One consequence was completely expected: my regular readership fell . . . precipitously. Another consequence was almost as expected: I reinvigorated my path to becoming a professional generalist. A final consequence was much less expected: I began to realize that I needed a new avenue to explore my generalist's approach to the world, and I needed to spend more time at home. I have Tori to thank.

CHAPTER 30

LENSES, LOOPS, AND LAGS

Despite my well-rounded thinking and generalist approach to navigating uncertainty, I had one obvious blind spot—well, it was obvious to everyone but me.

One Sunday night in the fall of 2016, Kai and Tori were upset. Tori came to me crying and asked, "Why do you have to go away every Sunday night?" Though my schedule was not as overwhelming as it had been in the hedge-fund days, it was still busy, especially with the demands of global speaking engagements and teaching the Yale class, which required me to drive back and forth to New Haven every week. Tori was direct and unsympathetic to my pleas of, "Sweetheart, it's where I work." She missed me, period.

Kai exerted a less direct plea. He was too young to understand the unfolding drama, but watching him content with Lego building and a widening group of friends at Torit, where he went to school, I realized that every hour I was away from the house, I was missing out.

It was heartbreaking.

Kristen, always tactful, suggested (with a sly smile) that there were some schools in the Boston area that might have equally capable students. And hadn't I enjoyed the shorter commute when spending time at the Kennedy School?

I resolved to find a way to be closer to the family. I began looking around for a teaching job near Boston. I was able to reconnect with Rakesh Khurana, dean of Harvard College. Rakesh and I had first met in 2002 when I was a graduate student at MIT Sloan and he was a young faculty member. He encouraged me to find a home at Harvard and offered to help. I didn't think it would be easy, but as a successful author with three graduate degrees and years of teaching popular courses at Yale, I didn't anticipate the hurdles I'd be required to leap to get a position. My first lesson: don't make a virtue of general expertise.

First, he pointed me toward Harvard's Economics Department. No dice. Though I'd worked in finance for almost twenty years, wrote a book and taught a class about financial bubbles, and had also done graduate work directly and indirectly on macro- and microeconomics with MIT's storied Economics Department, I was never really considered in some part because I was not an official, card-carrying PhD in economics. The same complaint was made by the Government Department. Yes, Vikram, they said, you have a master's degree in political science, but you're not a trained scholar in the field. Then we tried Sociology. Yes, they allowed, you've written about power dynamics and culture, but where's the PhD in sociology? The same dance occurred with Psychology. Okay, they conceded, you've written about behavioral biases and decision-making, but are you a psychologist? It was impossible if you didn't have the degree.

I was no stranger to the bureaucratic gatekeeping in higher education. Since my first introduction to Yale, administrators had been eager to put me in a box. And now, more than two decades later, armed with degrees in East Asian Studies; Ethics, Politics & Economics; Management; Security Studies; and Technological Innovation—not to mention a résumé filled with a diverse array of professional experiences—they were right back at it. After the psychologists said no, I was beginning to wonder if it was worth the bother. Academia was filled with round holes, and I was an octagonal peg. I just didn't fit.

Eventually, I ended up finding a position through a combination of Rakesh's savviness and sheer dumb luck. Rakesh introduced me to Frank Doyle, who at the time was the relatively new dean of Harvard's School of Engineering and Applied Sciences, and Rakesh felt he might be more open to new ideas. After I presented my pitch, Frank and his colleague Fawwaz Habbal sized me up: "You're a systems thinker," they noted. In their eyes, I was just applying an engineer's approach to human behavior. They appreciated my fascination with humanity amid uncertainty and thought I might be able to teach students to understand the toughest problems facing the planet via a systems approach. I'd written a book that took a multi-lens approach to finance, so we landed on the idea that I would teach a class that applied multi-lens approaches to other tough challenges.

And for the first time during this agonizing process, no one in the Engineering and Applied Sciences administrative offices questioned my credentials. Why? It turned out it was because I had a PhD from MIT. For engineers, MIT is Mount Olympus. Of course, no one really knew that my work was in innovation and entrepreneurship . . . and no one asked!

Fawwaz was excited enough about the course that he carved time out of his demanding schedule of being a dean, teaching classes, and running a research lab to design the course with me. I was thrilled, as he was one of the world's first inventors of a miniature camera to be placed in a cell phone and had run research for a major physics-oriented company. He even offered to join me as a co-instructor. Shortly thereafter, Cherry Murray also jumped in as an additional co-instructor, which was a huge benefit to the class because she was the prior dean of the School of Engineering and Applied Sciences; had run a large portion of Bell Labs, the legendary applied research facility associated with some of the world's most impactful innovations; and had just returned from Washington, DC, where she had served as the Department of Energy's chief scientist.

After months of design work, Fawwaz, Cherry, and I began teaching a course titled Humanity and Its Challenges: Systems Thinking Approaches to Harvard students in early 2017. In it, we analyzed some of the most complicated, pressing issues confronting nations around the world, such as how new technologies are affecting labor markets, the pressures mass migrations are putting on international borders, and how capitalism can exacerbate inequality.

I knew that each of these global challenges was being taken up by specialists in separate departments. Political scientists worried about migration and policy; economists worried about labor markets; historians concerned themselves with how the past informed capitalism and inequality. Indeed, every department at Harvard had some vantage point from which they approached how to explain and navigate humanity's challenges.

An explicit goal of my course was to teach students how to integrate disparate perspectives—or as my faculty colleagues might have said, think as a systems engineer. The goal was explicit: understand the complexity of the world as it is, not as it might appear from a particular discipline. What this meant was to introduce students to the skillful practice of how anyone can cycle through the insights of multiple experts to arrive at their own insights and recommendations. Implicitly, I was teaching these students that rather than reducing the complex to a single vantage point, they could acknowledge that complexity requires the agility of generalist thinking.

One of the best ways to teach system dynamics was the "beer game." No, it's not a drinking game played by students on weekends. It's an exercise designed to teach how everyone's perspective is limited, and it is only through a big-picture, holistic view that one can understand the dynamics of what is transpiring. The game is about the beer industry, and students are assigned to play different roles (some are retailers, some are distributors, some are producers, etc.). Communication between the different players is limited to mere "orders" for certain volumes to be delivered in the next period. Everyone has to figure out how much beer to order, and what inevitably occurs is that a minor increase or decrease in consumer demand compounds into a massive disturbance throughout the whole industry. Inventories disappear or surge, supplies are either plentiful or nonexistent, and the imperfect knowledge cascades into debilitating inefficiency and chaos. At the end of the exercise, students appreciate that no one did anything "wrong" per se, yet the system produced a horrible outcome. The lesson: analyzing the system is very different from analyzing the parts.

The class then went further, widening the lens beyond a simplified industry model seeking to make sure adequate supplies were in place. The issues faced by an industry (and all the companies within it) when navigating uncertainty could be similarly applied to a country or even a planet facing uncertainty at every level. Over time, I began suggesting a simple, three-step way for students to think about complex problems: (1) use **lenses** to identify relevant people, institutions, or factors; (2) identify how the parts interact with each other, with special attention to feedback **loops**; and (3) consider how **lags** could affect the time between a change in one component and the resulting change in another.

The cases were all chosen to demonstrate complexity, uncertainty, ambiguity, and unstable and dynamic relationships among the factors. We studied pandemics and how they could affect the world and societies or how technology and demographics were headed for a clash as robots impinged on labor markets. We addressed how climate change and energy policy interacted with food systems and shifting diets. And in one of the most intense cases, we studied capitalism and the impact of inequality on health, education, and a host of other topics.

To teach inequality, for instance, I would use my "lenses, loops, and lags" logic to guide the discussion. The class might begin with the understanding that capitalism is among the most powerful forces for good in the world, having improved the lives of billions. But we'd then describe how inequality is an existential risk to capitalism and how that inequality might spur other forms of economic organization, such as socialism. Then we'd see if we could understand why the system produced inequality and if there was a simple intervention we could make to help improve the situation by decreasing the impulse toward inequality.

Each time I led students through the inequality case, the pattern was almost the same. Education is the key, the students felt, to improving inequality. Give everyone a better education, and the disparities would dissipate. But then I'd ask, "How can we improve education?" Students were quick here: give poor-performing schools more resources. I'd chime in again, "But if education funding is dependent on local real estate taxes, how do you do that?" The class would then suggest that we needed to change housing and tax policy, possibly taking resources from the wealthier districts to give to the poorer ones.

"Okay, so let's imagine you just 'overpaid' for a house to move into a great school district, and you are also paying very high taxes to be in that town. How would you react if someone wanted to take money away from your children's school? What might happen to the value of your home?"

And on and on the discussion would go.

CHAPTER 31

MOVIES AND NOVELS?

Another teaching twist that I introduced in the class was that students were required to read novels and watch movies (not documentaries) about each case. The reason is that fiction helps expand the range of possibilities that we might consider. I believe it spurs creativity of thought and stirs the imagination in ways that mere facts cannot. At first, students were skeptical. One engineering student bluntly blurted out his concerns about my unconventional approach: "But novels are not true. Movies are not reality." My answer, of course, was "Not yet."

This was often met with incredulity. At which point, I asked them to imagine a story about an eight-hundred-foot-long luxurious, forty-five-thousand-ton ship that not only was capable of reaching 22.5 knots, driven by three propellers, but was also lauded by all as "unsinkable." I asked them to further imagine that the ship hit an iceberg in the North Atlantic, and due to an insufficient number of lifeboats, many passengers died when the vessel sank. I then added a romantic twist with one passenger falling in love with another. At this point, many students simply couldn't help themselves and chimed in with something along the lines of, "Yes, it's fiction, but the *Titanic* movie is about an actual event that happened in 1912. Fiction can be based on nonfiction events, but why should we read fiction when we can get the real story?"

Their jaws dropped when I told them that I was referring to an 1898 novel written by Morgan Robertson titled *Futility* (republished years later as *Wreck of the Titan*). The book, I reiterated, was written fourteen years *before* the actual *Titanic* sank and ninety-nine years before James Cameron's blockbuster movie hit the screens.

Robertson was no seer, just a serial novelist trying to hit on a bestseller. A minor note to the tragedy of the *Titanic*, which, of course, sank after hitting an iceberg in the North Atlantic, was that Robertson's book never found a mass general audience. Had it been the bestseller its author dreamed of, perhaps the subsequent voyage of the *Titanic* would have played out differently. I like to think, however, that at least one generalist in 1912 connected just enough disparate dots to pass on participating in the *Titanic*'s maiden voyage. Robertson's novel might have been just the nudge a prospective passenger might need in order to decide that an expert's "unsinkable" claim had not yet been substantiated—say, with one successful trip.

When it comes to more current events, I distinctly recall my students' reaction to *Contagion*, the 2011 movie about a pandemic that I had them watch for the case on humanity's risk of a global pandemic (a case I had designed in 2017, three years before the devastating coronavirus pandemic affected the world, and based on one of my annual predictions in 2015 that the world would face another global disease).

"It's just not realistic," the students complained. "It's so Hollywood! Conspiracy theories? Pushback against medical advice? Lockdowns? Not going to happen, ever." Sure, it seemed unlikely at the time, but that's the point. Many complex risks with huge ramifications are unlikely—that is, until they happen. I remember emphasizing to the class that year that the idea was to imagine what it might be like, not whether it was realistic. In fact, most of the cases were designed to teach students how to imagine different futures. And the measure of success that I held myself to was whether the exercise was useful in terms of spurring thoughts, changing preparations, managing risks, or spotting opportunities—not accuracy or likelihood. You see, as a generalist, imagination and creativity of thought about the future are very useful in navigating uncertainty, which is why I don't feel guilty when watching movies or reading fiction (and neither should you!).

Consider the novel I had students read for the inequality case: *Never Let Me Go*, by Nobel Prize–winning novelist Kazuo Ishiguro. The book presents several characters who exist solely because their organs can be used to keep others alive. As Ishiguro intended, readers are horrified. But when I share that there are accusations of similar scenarios, albeit far more scientifically nascent, currently happening in the world today, my students find themselves feeling beyond uncomfortable. What fiction and movies can do is push us into a zone of confusion and uncertainty, and for my students, that helped them think deeply about how to address very difficult problems, as well as how to evaluate the ramifications of doing nothing.

Every question raised and addressed in the class was a tough one. This was true for one obvious reason and one less obvious but more important reason. The obvious reason was in the name of the course, Humanity and Its Challenges. Less obvious was my intention to frustrate the students' ability to arrive at one indisputably correct solution. The power of the generalist—that there are many ways to understand, many solutions to weigh and pursue—can induce intellectual vertigo for the specialist. A specialist is a hammer seeking nails. A generalist carries around a toolbox. The very act of having a variety of tools leads one to view the world differently. "A short metal shaft with a flat top must be a nail" is the specialist's mantra, whereas a generalist will pause and ask questions. "Is the shaft threaded? Does the flat top have an indented slit? Or perhaps its top is a hexagon?" And with more answers, he reaches for a hammer, a screwdriver, or a wrench, depending on what he observes.

As much as my approach may have frustrated some of my students, I was always glad to be able to introduce them to tough questions that led to light-bulb moments and a healthy dose of humility. Uniformly, the students I had the pleasure of teaching at Harvard were bright. I was also glad to see that my class attracted students from a wide range of disciplines—only about a third in any given semester were enrolled in the School of Engineering and Applied Sciences. The other two-thirds came from every discipline, every department, across the college, and across the university's many schools. Smart, curious, and unspecialized undergraduates made up some of my best students. Almost by definition, they were all explorers. They had scoured the course offerings, landed on mine, and elected to journey across campus to my classroom. For many, the class was an elective, not required for the completion of their degree. What brought them to the course wasn't the need to check a box but simple curiosity.

One of the ironies of my academic pursuits is that the one type of institution that regularly asks me to teach its students is the one type of institution I least want to teach at: business schools. My experiences and education most suit me to teach MBA students, and business schools are less hidebound in their approach to hiring faculty. Still, it's not for me. The nature of graduate business schools is transactional. Unlike a PhD (which takes a minimum of four years and often takes seven), an MD (which also takes a minimum of four years and often takes seven), or a JD (which takes a minimum of three years), the two-year MBA degree can be a ticket-punch degree.

In my experience, MBA students, most of whom have already spent a few years on the fast track at management consulting firms, banks, or big corporations, are less interested than undergraduates in learning for learning's sake. Usually, they are back in school to accelerate their progress to the next, higher stage of their business careers. Or they are taking time from their fast-track careers to build a network or transition to a new role, geography, or industry. These students want a return on their investment measured in terms of career impact. It's a completely rational approach to the degree, and it works—just ask anyone holding an MBA from an elite business school.

But because teaching was only one part of my portfolio of activities, I really wanted to learn as much as I taught, and although I'm confident that can take place anywhere, I have personally found the interaction of a wide variety of students the most fulfilling. One of my favorite ways to force interaction and get students to see different perspectives is to organize debates. I often asked students to team up in pairs to debate another pair of students. I'd then give the foursome a topic (such as "Should we limit our use of fossil fuels?") and let them have a week or two to prepare. Except I'd add a unique twist: I didn't tell them which side of the debate they'd be arguing. They didn't get to choose, and they didn't know in advance. To be effective, therefore, the groups had to prepare both arguments. Generally, they did so, and usually did so very well, because their grades depended on it!

In one of these classes, I distinctly recall an art history major teamed up with a divinity school student to debate an applied physics doctoral candidate and a midcareer business school student. The debate was awesome, one of the most memorable of my teaching career, and a session from which I can honestly say I learned as much from the class as the students did. The morality of prioritizing an ever-changing climate at the expense of economic growth and human betterment was a hot topic, as was the possibility of geoengineering. Frankly, the class discussion was my first introduction to the idea of geoengineering and the potential benefits of using our understanding of physics, chemistry, and biology to control the atmosphere. There was even a question asked about how future generations might portray our society in art. Interactions like this were one reason I sought to spend time in classrooms for almost fifteen years.

CHAPTER 32

TORI LEADS THE WAY

What Kristen and I realized as we considered what was best for our family was the need to focus on *process* exclusively, accepting *outcomes*. As Tori's parents, this meant finding and making available the best circumstances where Tori's needs could be met. By 2017, Kristen was effectively Tori's dedicated Uber driver, chauffeuring her among a host of adaptive activities and therapists. Some of these helpers worked with us for such long periods of time that they became dear friends of the family. Others, however, came and went in the blink of an eye. We knew this wasn't optimal and that it couldn't continue, so we decided to look for a school that offered special educational services that could meet Tori's needs.

Lexington, Massachusetts, was brought to our attention as a suburban setting with a school system that prided itself on its special ed programs. We were able to find a nice house that all four of us liked. And indeed, the Lexington public school appeared to be perfect for Tori. Its special ed programs didn't clump all of its kids—with their wildly different needs—together, a terrible idea that was all too common when I was growing up. Instead, because Tori was very social, she was placed in a developmental learning program where she would be around other outgoing kids with similar learning disabilities.

Kai, a happy-go-lucky kid who would see little change to his schooling because he was still attending Torit, was fine with the move. But to preempt any potential anxiety, Kristen suggested we get Kai a dog. Not ever having been raised around dogs, I was reluctant. But after voicing my initial objections, ably countered by Kristen in a lovingly lawyer-like fashion, the contemplated possibility was "leaked," and we soon had a golden retriever puppy in the house, named "Douglas" by Kai after the road on which we lived. I was, eventually, also proved wrong on most of my objections by no greater expert than Douglas himself.

Life seemed promising. Kai had adjusted to the move without a hitch, and while the commute to Boston was longer for Kristen and Kai, they seemed to value the time together. And Kristen and I were optimistic with respect to Tori's education. We were in a town with great resources, including dozens of different instructors, each overseeing a sliver of Tori's individualized educational program (IEP). They had specialists addressing vision, behavior, speech, and physical and occupational therapies, and they boasted of special approaches to academic instruction. Sure, the town's taxes were commensurate with these services, but we hoped we'd found a partner community with a diverse array of experts who, collectively, would help.

But then, years of frustrations followed. Lexington was a picturesque community, though that was true of many Boston and Cambridge suburbs. We had deliberately sought out Lexington because of its schools and, specifically, the promise we thought they held for Tori. But with each passing year, we were dismayed to see that Tori had made little progress.

Part of the problem was that Tori was being siloed by each of these specialists. The adaptive physical education person focused on Tori's ability to navigate gym class and improve her executive functions, and the reading person was trying to help her read, but no one was tasked with integrating her education across these different domains. What was more, all the specialists generated a lot of paperwork, some of which tracked her progress, but only within an individual silo. Read each individual report, and her various experts professed progress. But year over year, Tori's IEP goals were never met. This fell to us to point out to the experts.

To call this frustrating is to put it kindly. Kristen and I were forced to sift through paper, put the same questions to different people, and told to trust the system. When we called out that the IEP goals hadn't been met over time, the wording of those goals was changed to conceal the fact. In one infuriating interchange, the reading specialist repeated, "We didn't get to that, and that's on me... sorry!" several times. Finally, Kristen and I had had enough. We confronted the dysfunction and confusion head-on. Despite being presented with the evidence, the school did not concur with our conclusion that Tori had made no progress in years. Therefore, we refused to sign off on the next IEP the school proposed. Instead, we asked them to place Tori in a different special needs school, which was also in Lexington but, like most schools of this type, required a "referral" from the student's district. In order to pursue this option for something different and perhaps better, we would need the Lexington school system to sign off.

We had compelling reasons to believe "different" really would mean "better." We had already seen the benefits of trying new approaches outside of Lexington. Tori had participated in adaptive sports—in which coaches trained in occupational therapy (OT) principles guide athletes—such as dancing, track, and even cheerleading, all of which built her confidence and were accompanied by some degree of success. But one day, Rachel, one of Tori's friends from gymnastics, had just returned from a resort in New Hampshire where she had tried to ski. Her mother, Julie, nudged us to take Tori.

One of Tori's challenges at the time was that she lacked, in the language of the OT community, "proprioceptive" sense—meaning she really didn't appreciate where her body was in space. Adaptive sports offered a fun way to address this particular challenge.

Kristen had always been a fan of skiing, having acquired her fair share of skiing trophies during her youth. She had wanted all of us to learn how to ski, but it had proved an uphill battle. Kristen's first attempt to get Tori on the slopes resulted in several injuries on the first day. But Kristen persisted, this time bringing Kai, who took to the sport like a fish to water. With the experience of sharing the love of the sport with Kai, Kristen really wanted Tori to learn.

To be honest, I was the problem. I was scared of getting hurt, nervous about injuring someone else on the slopes, and genuinely concerned about highlighting another activity that Tori couldn't enjoy. Yes, I had skied several times, and I'd even joined Kristen on a ski vacation while we were dating, but that was because I wanted to be with her, not because I enjoyed or even wanted to be on the slopes.

I had my doubts. Kristen was animated by hope. And Kai was always game to ski. We followed Julie's advice and reached out to the New Hampshire resort.

There is no way Kristen or I thought that taking Tori up to Loon Mountain for a weekend of lessons with the New England Disabled Sports (NEDS) program would change our lives. Yet that's exactly what happened, and we have to thank Julie for the initial push.

NEDS is an amazing program that started in 1987 as White Mountain Adaptive Snow Sports and began with six volunteers, including the two founders, Dr. Bob Harney and Emily Morrison. Since then, the program has grown to more than 250 dedicated and highly trained volunteers and conducts thousands and thousands of lessons each year. And it's no longer restricted to just winter sports—summer programming includes golf, archery, rock climbing, paddleboarding, biking, pickleball, and kayaking. In addition, the athlete pool today comprises children and adults with physical and cognitive challenges and has helped people of all types to participate in sports activities. Individuals who are blind, deaf, and autistic learn alongside disabled veterans who might lack limbs.

I would try absolutely anything that might help Tori to get more active and to help her master new ways of navigating the world. Julie had passed along information about a scholarship program that would give us an on-mountain hotel room, lift tickets for the whole family, and four lessons for Tori over the weekend. To Kristen and me, this spoke volumes. It was clear that on top of being an amazing opportunity for kids, the NEDS program sought to include families based on fit, not means. In a real, measurable way, program and mountain were doing their part, and we leaped at the chance to try it out. Kristen and Kai were thrilled. Compared to Nashoba, the glorified hill where Kai had learned to ski, Loon was a virtual Everest. They'd ski while Tori took a lesson, and I'd watch and take pictures of Tori coming down the hill.

Understandably, Kristen and I have always been protective of Tori. Too often, we've encountered experts—very often in positions of influence at local schools—who've implicitly approached her and us as a problem in need of a solution. We always rejected this, of course, as it throws up a barrier; it creates separation. Worse, it ignores a universal truth: all of us share more in common than what differentiates us.

I'd always struggled with the "special needs" label. Not because I think it is stigmatizing but because I think it applies to everyone. Hell, without a doubt, it had applied to me. I needed Mrs. Buffett, I needed Jack Bogle, I needed my swimming coaches at Blair, John Meeks to get me through Physics 260, and on and on. It was only when I kicked up against some organization—say, Yale—that saw me as a problem, a son of immigrants in need of help, and then tried to foist on me a solution, the Pre-Registration Orientation Program, that I got angry. Programs like PROP and the logic that supports them turn inclusion into something condescending and harmful.

The migrant mindset, however, understands that inclusion is a two-way street, a guest-and-host relationship. No matter what you bring to the party, you need to be open to new relationships—that's what being a good guest means. And if others open themselves up to you, you are given the opportunity to be a good host. Guest and host are two sides of the same coin. Inclusion should be an experience of adding to, not conforming to. But not every community works this way, and that means when you open yourself to a new community, you give the responsibility of inclusion to someone else.

What was so amazing about New Hampshire and the community we found in Lincoln was that our fears instantly proved groundless. That first weekend at the mountain, the entire family experienced tremendous joy. Despite not really being able to stand on skis—let alone make it to the bunny hill or even the least threatening means of getting up a slope, the magic carpet (think of a conveyor belt for skiers)—Tori beamed. The only pictures I had taken that day were of Kai and Kristen skiing, but the image of Tori's smile is indelibly lodged in my memory. The volunteers were happy, upbeat, encouraging, and supportive. They were knowledgeable, persistent, and dedicated. A good experience, for sure, but my initial conclusion was, "Glad we tried it, but skiing may not be for Tori."

Weeks later, Tori asked to go back, so we did, much to Kai's and Kristen's joy. And we did again. And again. By the end of that first season, Tori had managed to stand on skis and maybe even move about five to ten feet without falling. Not a huge accomplishment, but she was happy, and both Kristen and I had noticed a growing interest on her end—which we remain convinced was due to the community, not necessarily the skiing. Nevertheless, the next season, we returned almost every weekend. Kai was now developing into a serious skier, Kristen was enjoying time with him, and I happily played the role of sherpa and driver.

It was toward the end of that season that Tori was able to come down Sarsaparilla, the bunny hill at Loon Mountain, by herself. Hooray! The accomplishment proved to be both a huge confidence boost for her and a major inflection point for me. Tori proudly proclaimed to me, "Daddy, I'm learning!" I was so proud of her, but then she added, "You can, too!"

Telling Tori, who had struggled with learning almost anything, that I was afraid was not an option. So the next day, I began taking lessons, and although I fell several times on a beginner slope, I was thrilled to see Kai and Kristen pointing at me, giggling, as they rode the chairlift. Tori was amused by the snow all over my jacket, despite the fact it wasn't snowing that day. The rest, as they say, is history.

I'm pleased to say that I've turned into a slow but confident skier and now feel comfortable going down any trail on any mountain!

Our feeling of joy snowballed as we got to know other families who were part of the community. All of us, at some level, allowed ourselves to trust each other and be vulnerable with this part of our lives. And Tori felt this joy more than anyone. She became outspoken, more confident, and more willing to interact with others. She was a different person in Lincoln, New Hampshire, than she was in Lexington, Massachusetts. We attributed this to the great sense of collective support and care that emanated from the wonderful people who made all of us feel comfortable and welcome.

CHAPTER 33

THE KAI GUY SHOW

Our desire to move Tori from the Lexington School District into another program was influenced by the great strides she made with the NEDS programs. So, we approached the school that spring about outplacement options. At this point, we encountered yet another specialist, the head of special ed for the entire Lexington district. I'm not exactly sure what her ostensible area of expertise was, but it clearly wasn't the well-being of students. In fact, after several increasingly unpleasant encounters, Kristen and I concluded this woman's job must have been to make sure that no outplacements would ever occur so that resources were not taken from the Lexington schools and the district's reputation as a place that could handle anything wasn't undermined . . . or so it seemed.

The more we pushed up against it, the more Kristen and I found our conviction that money should flow to students, not schools. If a school met the needs of a student, great. If not, a student should have the choice to opt for a school that better fit his or her needs. We were blessed to have two wonderful children, but they were very different learners. And of the hundreds of kids Kristen has seen progress through Torit, there were dozens and dozens of learning styles. Heck, I saw the same thing at Yale, MIT, and then Harvard. Kids deserve better than a one-size-fits-all approach to education. And this, ultimately, was why we became strong proponents of school choice.

Ironically, the teachers who worked most closely with Tori agreed that their program wasn't right for her. No matter. The bureaucrat who managed the program still attempted to block our efforts to move Tori to something more suited to her needs. To add insult to injury, Kristen and I learned that this administrator was paid multiples of the amount the well-intentioned teachers were paid.

Three things then happened at roughly the same time that would have a huge impact on our family. First, Tori skipped much of the traditional extended school year program (summer school) in Lexington and spent it with the NEDS program in Lincoln. The differences in approach were stark. The Lexington occupational and physical therapists broke her physical skills down into component tasks; for example, they would ask her to walk on the line in a school gym and the like. Her NEDS volunteers, on the other hand, would take her out to the middle of Mirror Lake in Thornton, New Hampshire, and have her stand on a paddleboard. The Lexington experts' approach to improving Tori's bilateral coordination took place in a therapy room. NEDS put her in a kayak, where, after going in a circle for a while, Tori figured out that bilateral effort might be more productive. The increased confidence from these small successes led Tori to a willingness to try to learn things, such as waterskiing. The range of what Tori was interested in and willing to attempt grew, and with it, programs were there to help her. Less "expertise" was proving useful; Tori was figuring it out and doing things that no one back in Lexington had thought were possible.

The second thing to happen was that Kristen and I began to seriously consider legal action against Lexington to provide us with the outplacement we'd need to get Tori appropriate schooling. We knew we could build a strong case based on the accumulated data of the school's failure, and with a Harvard-educated literally in-house counsel representing us, we were confident in the likely outcome. But the idea of going legally toe-to-toe with the system we were asking to help undertake her education seemed counterproductive. What was the best-case outcome? A court victory, a pissed-off school, and Tori confronting the blowback? So we decided that this was not the best option for anyone, particularly Tori. A legal battle with the Lexington School District was not going to increase Tori's happiness or help her flourish.

The third and final thing that happened was a realization on my part of the most humbling lesson I learned about myself and my family during those years. In trying to help Tori, I had lost sight of the lesson I had worked hard to impart to all those Harvard students. The power of the generalist was the insight and eventual mastery of a multi-lens way of understanding that allowed you to see many solutions to a possible challenge or problem. It dawned on me that I hadn't yet allowed myself to be a generalist toward my kids. I had remained a dad ever hopeful that there was some trained expert out there with some unique insight that would make things easier for Tori. More shameful, as I had gone ever deeper down the rabbit hole of experts for Tori, I had been less engaged with Kai than I wanted to be. Like lots of parents, I had my reasons, a laundry list of obligations and commitments that were pressing. And for me, none of that rolled up to a sufficient explanation.

What made this all the more confounding for me is that starting in 2018, then full-time in 2019, I was writing another book, this one titled *Think for Yourself: Restoring Common Sense in an Age of Experts and Artificial Intelligence*. It was written with a business-book-buying audience in mind, but as I drafted and polished chapters on the promise and perils of focus and outsourced thinking, the need to triangulate perspectives, and what self-reliance in the twenty-first century required, I realized each and every one of these insights worked at home. If, of course, I paid attention. I became so excited at this connection—thinking for yourself applied to home and office—I spelled it out to my editor at the publishing house that had acquired the book. Not only did he push back; he made it clear he intended to determine the title, content, and scope and focus of the book's marketing. I will never forget his attempt to claim control by asserting his expert status.

"Vikram, trust us. This is a business book for managers," he told me. "We're the experts here."

Given that I had titled one chapter of the manuscript "Keep Experts on Tap, Not on Top," I couldn't help but laugh. In short order, we worked out an amicable separation, and I found a new and better partner for the book, Harvard Business Review Press.

Everywhere I looked, I began to ask myself, *Okay, thinking for myself and following my own advice, what can and ought to change? What needs to be attempted?* And I distinctly remember making a New Year's resolution on January 1, 2020, to be a different dad ASAP.

The question was, How? Tori needed our constant focus, with a consequence being that there was lots of time to forge an evolving relationship with her. By founding her own school, Kristen had created an immersive way to braid her professional interest with being with the kids. Once Tori had moved beyond Torit Montessori, I had made my role in her life revolve around experts, medical and educational, and my search for a just-right solution. Under the "only so many hours in a day" rule, I had given other parts of my life insufficient attention. Now I was determined to find a way to strengthen and deepen my relationship with Kai, our precocious nine-year-old.

He and I had always enjoyed being together, but I realized that nine is a new, more curious age. Each day, he was more and more his own person, and I wanted to be a bigger part of that transition. Simple logistics meant that he still spent a lot more time with Kristen than with me. The two of them drove to Boston each school day so that Kai could attend Torit while Kristen worked there.

Kristen, always very supportive, helped me come up with a plan. Starting in January, I'd take Kai skiing at different mountains throughout New Hampshire, using the opportunity to spend more time with him. Sadly, that didn't work. Kai had his own priorities and was determined to commit his free skiing time to the Loon Race Team. But then something completely unexpected happened.

I was sitting at my desk in my home office, trying to figure out GarageBand, the audio-editing software that comes with Apple computers. Kai wandered in, saw what I was attempting, and asked the obvious question, "What are you doing?"

I quickly explained why I was spending time learning about making recordings that sound good. In anticipation of the release of my forthcoming book, *Think for Yourself*, I was learning how to create and launch a podcast.

Kai nodded thoughtfully and looked at my computer screen. "Do you know what you're doing?"

"Well, not really. Right now, I'm trying to figure it out. Wanna help?"

This is not as odd a question to put to a nine-year-old as you might expect. As a digital native, Kai had become our extended family's in-house tech support, often helping Kristen or grandparents with their phone settings, computer hiccups, and generally anything run by a central processing unit.

He agreed to try to help me with GarageBand, and we spent the next hour or so figuring out how to trim audio clips, add in background music, modulate volumes, and even combine files. We decided to experiment a bit with a conversation between us, and lo and behold, it worked! We (though mostly Kai) had figured it out. I thanked him, and then, almost as a throwaway question, I asked, "Do you want to launch a podcast also?"

"Sure," he said without any hesitation. "That'd be fun!" So we began working to help each other out with our respective podcasts. He helped me post the trailer to *The Think for Yourself Podcast* on January 27, 2020, and then I helped him post the introductory episode of *The Kai Guy Show* on January 28, 2020. We had a blast.

One of the most memorable parts of helping him launch his show was the first time we recorded. I promised him that this was going to be fun, so we didn't use scripts. I put the mic in front of him, and as soon as I hit the record button, he blurted out, "This is Kai Guy..."

Kai Guy? I mean, I get it. *Mansharamani* can seem a mouthful, but he'd been saying it for his entire life. He noticed my confusion, paused the recording, and began to explain himself. His time in the car listening to the radio while Kristen drove led him to believe that people needed "radio names." Something memorable, easily repeatable, something like, well, Kai Guy.

After shrugging, I smiled, which he took as acceptance. He resumed the recording, allowing our unscripted session to capture his stream-of-conscious communication: "This is Kai Guy coming in live, but by the time you hear this, well, it won't really be live, so I guess I'm coming in *not* live."

I was proud, confused, and definitely amused. Kai again paused the recording to bring me along, explaining the asynchronous nature of podcasting. It was both spontaneous but not, he claimed. A podcast was a live recording, but most listeners wouldn't hear it for hours or days or even years after it had been recorded. I nodded along with a big smile, thinking about how foreign these concepts would have been to me at his age.

I was beaming. And just as had proven true for Tori learning from real-life activities, Kai enjoyed ancillary benefits from his podcast. Kristen and I loved watching Kai improve his organizational skills as he prepared for each interview. And as he improved his ability to edit the podcasts, we watched his composition and essay-writing skills improve in tow.

I distinctly recall the moment I couldn't make the Lexington dots connect anymore. Kristen and I had returned to Massachusetts for one of Tori's IEP meetings at the school, and we walked into a formal conference room with dozens of experts, all of whom were armed with credentials that justified their positions. One after another, they all talked about how they knew exactly what Tori needed. This therapy for speech, that therapy for dexterity, another therapy that covered someone else's individual specialty. But no one was tying it all together to explain how it would help Tori as a person, and no one was admitting that all of their insights had produced little to no progress over the past five years. Maybe they knew their siloed domains of knowledge better than we did, but Kristen and I clearly knew Tori best and had ideas of our own. Trying to help Tori was our goal, but being in conflict with the experts in the room felt lousy. Worse, we had no interest in battling this room full of experts for control of Tori's education.

At some point, it just hit us. Why not form our lives around the blissful New Hampshire existence? Kristen and I, with the help of friends in New Hampshire, decided to jump into the Lincoln community that had been so open to receiving us and had worked so well for Tori. I was fortunate to have the professional flexibility to work remotely, and the extra hours I'd spend going to and from the airport when traveling were a minor inconvenience placed against our family's comfort in being part of a welcoming community.

Kristen confronted a harder choice. To be with Tori in Lincoln would require a career- and life-changing decision: hire professionals to take her place at a job she loved, running the school she'd built. For many years, she had skillfully taken care of more than one hundred children and, perhaps even more consequentially, almost two hundred parents. This was never truer than with the onset of COVID. Responding to the health crisis had required ongoing inventiveness with staff, curricula, and technology. But she'd managed it—and brilliantly. Kristen has her own set of generalist skills that wouldn't be easily replaced. But we put our children first and committed to the move.

In 2020, we decided to make Lincoln our year-round home. As Kristen reorganized her involvement with Torit, which became a real-time experiment in answering the question of how many specialists you needed to replace one exceedingly capable generalist, I knew my objective was not only to make myself a skilled generalist at home. It was also to raise two young generalists in New Hampshire.

CHAPTER 34

WHY LIVE ANYWHERE ELSE?

During the years my family has lived in New Hampshire, I've come to deeply appreciate the state motto, proudly posted on each license plate: "Live Free or Die." After all, to live free is the essence of the migrant mindset and closely mirrors the generalist's creed of "Think free and stay open-minded." To fully fit my message, however, you would need a license plate big enough to include the following: "Think freely, speak freely, listen freely, and be free to do your part." Everywhere, everyone we encountered in New Hampshire seemed to be living according to this creed. For Kristen, Tori, Kai, and me, this translated simply into, Why live anywhere else? New Hampshire is a wonderful place to be a generalist.

Our transition was so natural, it took me a while to understand how it happened. The migrant mindset favors exploration and being both guest and host. Throughout my life, I'd received its benefits as it helped me join new communities that nurtured and sustained me, sometimes at crucial moments. In the places where I have most readily felt at home, I found others who were equally interested in respecting and learning from each other. This is the essence of a happy community, where each member contributes their unique knowledge, skills, and gifts in a spirit of giving and receiving. Whether it was at Blair, Bear Stearns, the Willard, or countless other stops along the way, I had experienced the power of this dynamic in action. But

I had never felt such a profound sense of home and community as I felt watching Tori ski down the mountain among amazingly kind and caring people we'd only recently met.

It wasn't just evident on the mountain of a ski resort. In New Hampshire, I noticed that the roots of collective support ran deep. Perhaps it was due to the state's commitment to limited government? Might big government "crowd out" community spirit as individuals come to expect the government to solve their problems? Regardless as to why, it was real.

This New Hampshire spirit is embodied in Heather Krill, an inspirational figure we met in Lincoln who quickly became a dear friend (and uphill skiing companion who also enjoyed the fitness climbs to traverse the opposite direction of most!). A local English teacher and author of *True North*, a young adult novel, Heather helped us integrate into local Lincoln life, introducing us to just about everyone in town (and she knows just about everyone!). Helping people is her way—her husband, Geoff, was paralyzed and confined to a wheelchair after a serious accident, and they have two children. She jumps in to help whenever, wherever, and however needed. That's just how she is—she treats her responsibility to other people as a higher calling. The concept of guest and host has, for Heather, become something more basic: we are all in this together. And Geoff has such an awesome can-do attitude that he became one of the world's best-seated skiers and runs an adaptive waterskiing program during the summers (not to mention he's also a sought-after speaker on topics around leadership and resilience!).

Contrasts were everywhere. Unlike the individualized education program meetings in Massachusetts, in which Kristen and I were told the experts knew what was best for our daughter, the first IEP meeting in Lincoln was a refreshing change. We sat around a table in the cafeteria with Georgia Cady, a charming, kind, and energetic woman who drove a Volkswagen Bug and was probably armed with more experience and knowledge than any Massachusetts expert. She began our meeting with words that brought tears of joy to our eyes:

"You know Tori best. What do we need to best enable her success?" (In fact, even typing these words is overwhelmingly emotional.) Kristen and I knew our instincts were right, that we had indeed found a place that respected us as parents and also prioritized our daughter. This was the both-and logic we sought. The contrast with prior IEP meetings was overwhelming.

I've come to appreciate that New Hampshire encourages us to answer this calling, this understanding of our common humanity. The reciprocal sense of what neighbor can do for neighbor is vital in rural areas. As Georgia, who lives in Coos County, a sparsely populated part of New Hampshire that is north of Franconia Notch and is part of the "North Country," once pointed out to me: "When the snow gets to be several feet high and I've dug myself out, the first thing I do is help dig out my neighbor. And they do the same for me. We have to work together; otherwise, we're not going to survive."

I had followed a winding path to a career as a professional generalist. My parents had gifted me with a strong start, encouraging a migrant mindset and instilling the common courtesy of both guest and host. Starting with Blair but continuing through Yale and MIT, educational opportunities had allowed me to research and think about the practices and tools to better navigate uncertainty. I had also discovered that I could forge a career as a professional generalist, whether working for a hedge fund or working for myself. It was in New Hampshire, however, that I first fully appreciated that the path needn't be crooked and that being a generalist was more encompassing than just a profession. Being a generalist could, and ought to, be a way of being.

With the help of Lincoln's remarkable people, we settled into our new life. And for the first time since we'd had kids, the family felt stable. The kids were happy. Though Kristen had recruited a team to run Torit, she was often pulled back into helping from Lincoln. She worked remotely but also undertook the two-and-a-half-hour drive to Boston as needed. She had an entrepreneur's commitment to the school she had founded, as well as something more profound:

she ardently believed in its mission and purpose and the good it was doing for children and families. Tori and Kai had been beneficiaries, and she wanted this possibility to be available for others.

I was working from home; going back and forth to teach at Harvard, making a weekly trek to the campus; and continuing to work as a consultant and public speaker. But living in Lincoln and watching Kristen's commitment to a larger purpose spurred me to think hard about what more I could do for the community I had joined. I was serving as a Trustee of the Trust Fund for the town but was eager to do more. And around that time, a few dear long-standing friends started suggesting that I run for political office.

Well, not everyone. I remember telling my friend Lori Robinson, a retired four-star general and former commander of the North American Aerospace Defense Command (NORAD) who is originally from New Hampshire, about my emerging plan. "We're really settled in now, and everything is going smoothly," I told her. "Tori and Kai are happy. Kristen loves it here. I think it is a place where I can, I should, give back." Pausing to weigh my words, I said, "I think I'm in a place now where I might be able to serve in public office. I'm trying to find a way I can help the country that attracted my family and gave me so many opportunities."

"So you're telling me everything's good," she said with a smile on her face. "Well, then, why mess it up by going into politics?" While she was encouraging, she was also asking an honest and important question.

I laughed nervously, recognizing she had hit a nerve. Is it too reductive to say that watching a community fully accept my family was enough of a reason to take a risk on politics and possibly upset the apple cart? Maybe. Yes, the people and place were inspiring and provided a compelling reason to volunteer as a trustee and consider donating my time to local service groups. But I had to admit to myself that the pull toward politics had something larger at its core. America's rapidly escalating tensions with China, which I believe to be one of the central foreign-policy issues of our time, also strongly influenced my thinking. Over the past decade, the United States had been increasingly looking inward. We'd become so focused on our cultural disagreements, we'd overlooked some of America's biggest external threats. This had come at a grave cost to our national security, especially with respect to China.

While political extremists devoted most of their energy to making villains out of each other, China had stolen trade secrets, extorted corporations to give up proprietary technologies, engaged in brazen espionage, aggressively expanded its military, and used its wealth and power to subvert America's international interests. At the same time, under Xi Jinping's leadership since 2013, China's government had become ever more centralized, intrusive, authoritarian, and controlling of every facet of Chinese life. The China that had killed thousands of protesting citizens in Tiananmen Square in 1989 was now the China committing genocide against its Uyghur population in East Turkestan.

I found the increasingly autocratic Chinese Communist Party and the willingness of its dictator to pursue a course of conflict with the world's democracies alarming. With my background, it was also an area where I felt I had something significant to offer. I'd been thinking seriously about China and its role in the world since I was an undergraduate at Yale. From my first formal study of the country under the tutelage of Ambassador James Lilley to my time working at the US embassy in Beijing and writing about China under the guidance of Paul Kennedy and Paul Bracken, I had developed a breadth and depth of awareness that I wanted to use to help my country. It was game time in the US-China relationship, and I was looking for a way to get off the bench.

CHAPTER 35

COIN OF THE REALM

My time at the Kennedy School had introduced me to impressive and accomplished professionals, many of whom had done "tours of duty" in Washington, DC, serving the nation as policymakers, diplomats, or in other leadership roles. I was always impressed by their selflessness and willingness to serve America. I found my peers quite inspiring in this regard. Over coffee one day in 2019, while attending a meeting of the Faculty Working Group on Technology and Public Policy, I asked a colleague who'd spent time in business, academia, and government which he had enjoyed the most and where he'd felt most impactful. He was too smart to answer the question directly but provided extraordinary insight that has stuck with me.

"Vikram, the key to success in academia, or elsewhere, is very simple," he told me. "You must acquire the coin of the realm. In academia, the coin of the realm is a full-tenure position. This means you have obtained not only the security of tenure but all the reputational prestige that comes from a career that has resulted in tenure."

"But I have no interest in being a full-time academic," I replied.

"Same is true everywhere. If you go work for Fidelity," he went on, "the coin of the realm is to produce profits as a portfolio manager. The most successful portfolio manager holds the coin of the realm and is able to effect the most change."

He was right. Though for most of my career, I had been valued by others because I stood outside of their siloed realms. That had been a truism of my professional life. Again and again, I had been invited by individuals who held the coins of their realm to come in to speak, advise, and teach. My input was valued, but clearly as a supporting actor. I wondered, *In what realm does a generalist hold the most coin? Where can a generalist do the most good? Might it be in the realm of public service?*

"What about politics?" I asked him. "What's the coin of the realm in government?"

He paused. I imagined him running through a series of glib, cynical answers: money, influence, power. But he surprised me.

"In a democracy, or representative government, the coin of the realm is elected office and the corresponding ability to advance the most good for constituents."

As he said these words to me, something clicked. Elected public office might, in fact, be where a generalist would be best positioned to do the most good. This reasoning, I knew at the time, was far from a sufficient motive to run, however. A few other pieces would have to fall into place first. And without my seeking them out, they did.

Kristen and I had been attending the National Finals Rodeo (NFR) in Las Vegas with Jim Timmerman and his extended family for years. We were introduced to a couple who knew the Timmermans well: Rachel and Clarence Werner. Clarence "CL" Werner was the founder of Werner Enterprises, one of the largest trucking companies in the United States. He'd taken a company initially run out of his home with one truck and turned it into a multibillion-dollar corporation with around ten thousand trucks, a true Horatio Alger story if ever there was one. It turned out that CL and Rachel were also some of the most active political donors in the country. Rachel, who is charming, politically astute, and very much eager to see change, kept nudging me to run for office.

"You've got good ideas," she'd tell me. "You've gotta run, Vikram." And every year, I'd reply, "No, thanks. Not for me."

And every year, I'd meant it—that is, until late 2021. I can point to many reasons, but here are a few events that shifted my thinking: the US's fraught relationship with China was worsening, something I saw not just in my research and the news but also in my professional backyard. I saw a Harvard professor pulled out of his lab in handcuffs because of the illegal work he was doing for the Chinese government.

My decision to run came to a head after the popular governor of New Hampshire, Christopher Sununu, announced in late 2021 that he would not run for the US Senate. Suddenly, a bunch of people, both in and outside New Hampshire, began encouraging me to throw my hat into the ring, making some of the same arguments I'd been thinking about myself.

"Vikram, the country needs unity, not division. You're good at this."

"Vikram, we need someone who understands how the economy works as well as the threat posed by China and Russia."

"Vikram, we need an agile thinker to deal with all this uncertainty."

And there was something else people kept saying to me: "New Hampshire needs a freethinker who isn't going to blindly go along with all the 'experts' in Washington."

It was wonderful to be seen as an open-minded generalist, something I'd worked so long and hard to become. To be characterized as a free and agile thinker was music to my ears. That's not to say that I don't have strong opinions. I do. I believe strongly in limited government, personal responsibility, and clearly asserted and strongly supported national interests. I hold a bedrock faith in freedom, opportunity, and accountability, grounded in equality under the law. I also have a deep commitment to open, civil discourse that appreciates every human's potential for a needle-moving contribution. This, too, is a bedrock belief.

I have frequently been both a good guest and a good host who has openly listened to opinions that I do not necessarily share. I approach all discourse with courtesy because that's how the flow of ideas works best. This sort of civility is born out of a steadfast belief that whatever our differences, all Americans share common good intentions. The energy of a fruitful debate lies in the friction created by a variety of opinions, ideas, and perspectives. But friction can't happen unless everyone is working together. Screaming matches don't create friction, only noise. I've never been interested in making noise. Crafting messages, ideas, and innovations that break through the noise—now *that* is interesting to me. So, I was thrilled to be encouraged to enter politics not just because of my beliefs and ideas but because of the *way* I thought and engaged with other people's beliefs and ideas.

One of the reasons I'd never seriously entertained running before was because it seemed unlikely that someone with a long last name with a lot of syllables like *Mansharamani* was going to be a viable candidate in a state that was more than 96 percent white. In reality, this didn't seem to matter in New Hampshire. The people I spoke to all over the state never made me feel like my ethnicity or last name was a factor. Frankly, I was wrong and closed-minded to even think it was an issue.

I had long wanted to contribute and give back to my country and the people of New Hampshire, who had welcomed my family with open arms. A few people early on indicated that they were willing to help get my campaign finances up and running. And perhaps most importantly, more and more people in New Hampshire—the very people who would be my constituents—were enthusiastic about the prospect of me representing them. And more generally, New Hampshire, its ethos and spirit, its creed of "Live free or die," resonated with my beliefs. With Kristen, Kai, and Tori offering their support, I decided to jump into the primary for the US Senate and see how it would go.

When I said I was running as a Republican, many eyebrows went up. Even those who'd known me for a long time were unsure about my party affiliation. And frankly, if I had announced myself as a Democrat, my guess is that more eyebrows would have been raised. The main reason for the confusion, I believed, was that I was not a politician. I'd never thought in partisan or political terms. I'd never written or spoken in a manner that telegraphed a particular party allegiance. Heck, I was a self-described independent thinker and had even written a book encouraging readers to think for themselves.

When I was growing up, my parents were too busy trying to make ends meet to be politically active beyond regularly voting. They always voted for a person rather than a party, and because of their immigrant heritage, they disproportionately cared about foreign affairs. One of my earliest political memories is my father saying that a weak president—Jimmy Carter—was the reason Iran took Americans hostage, a logic that was indelibly burned into my memory when the Islamic Republic released them minutes after Ronald Reagan's inauguration. Did that make him a dyed-in-the-wool Republican? Absolutely not. Over the years, he'd voted Democrat, Republican, as well as for and against the same candidate in different elections. My mother, a member of a health-care workers union, leaned toward being a Democrat, but I recall that she liked President Reagan, President George W. Bush, and President Bill Clinton—an eclectic mix.

Given my generalist approach and fiercely independent thinking, party affiliation was, for me, about underlying values. And in that respect, the guiding principles on topics that mattered most to me aligned me squarely with the Republican Party. A belief in peace through strength. Disdain for centralized authority that encroaches on individual liberties. And like families around the country do every week, I believe governments should live within their means. These values are supplemented by a strong faith in America's entrepreneurial spirit and a belief that less government will unleash individual creativity and improve the lives of many.

My parents, understandably, were super proud that I wanted to serve my country. They didn't really care if I won or lost; they were simply impressed by my willingness to try. They asked when I would publicly declare my candidacy, and when I told them it would be soon, my dad overnighted some important documents. The day before I declared my candidacy, an Express Mail envelope arrived containing both of my parents' naturalization certificates. They'd been in my father's safe-deposit box for decades. My dad wanted me to remember that this country really was a land of opportunity and that among the rising tide of xenophobia, it was critical to remember that America was, is, and should always remain a shining city upon a hill.

My political announcement video was, in many ways, the embodiment of my generalist thinking and a statement that experts should remain on tap, not on top. After discussing the challenges Kristen and I had with Tori's education—when experts repeatedly told us to sit down, keep quiet, and do what they said—I simply stated:

> I'm running because it's time the experts sit down and listen to us. Let's be honest, where did blindly following these so-called experts get us? It got us record inflation, budget-busting gas prices, an exploding mental health crisis, and a world in which borders are not respected. Two weeks to flatten the curve turned into two years that flattened the middle class. We've gone from energy independence to importing oil from those who hate us.

The announcement video lasted two minutes and provided a quick overview of my position on the major issues. I was excited about the prospects of serving the people of New Hampshire to the best of my abilities and looked forward to hearing their ideas and working collaboratively to address their needs. It was with that spirit of learning about the challenges faced by Granite Staters that I kicked off my campaign.

CHAPTER 36

RETAIL POLITICS 101

One of the first things I realized when I became a full-time candidate is that everyone has an opinion about everything, especially people in New Hampshire. People would tell me, "Vikram, you know, you might be more senatorial if you part your hair on the other side. Or maybe you should wear khaki jeans? Or blue jeans? Have you ever thought about black jeans?" To be honest, outside of putting together my country-western wardrobe for the rodeo, I hadn't ever really spent much time thinking about jeans before. Or what winter vest I should wear or how my hair was done.

Presentation and image projection are, of course, undeniably important in running for office. Anyone who has put on a power suit to give a presentation understands the concept. But there is something unhealthy about our cultural obsession with largely superficial matters when it comes to selecting officeholders. Our world of around-the-clock political coverage, which spends a lot of time on polls, horse-race stories, and insider talk about the latest political gossip, has not been healthy for our democracy.

The unsolicited campaign advice wasn't only about my appearance. Whereas many approached the advice-giving from a place of "Think freely, speak freely, listen freely, and then, Vikram, make up your mind," a growing number of professionals offered expert advice. Politics, it turned out, had spawned an entire industry of consultants and advisers for every aspect of running a campaign, including policy analysis, media buying, image management, and digital campaigning. Many people also had thoughts on how I should express myself. "You ought to talk more about this and less about that. Do you know your website doesn't look great? And that tweet you sent? It should have been worded differently."

Issues mattered, without question. But so, too, did jeans and haircuts or the color of the background on my Instagram profile picture. And those currently holding office provided stories about their experiences. Everyone seemed to be an expert in something, and with that expertise came prescriptions and advice. It seemed like every single human being I interacted with told me how I could do things differently and better and that they had cracked the code for running for office. It would take me a while to realize that in politics, keeping experts on tap, not on top, was not easy.

In New Hampshire, though, politicians have good reasons to listen. Granite Staters can claim to have cracked the code with more credibility than most. One reason they are so attuned to politics, of course, is because of the state's importance as an early primary state in presidential elections. New Hampshire is immersed in retail politics. Another reason is that, aware of their importance, the residents take the responsibility seriously. They express interest and expect that interest to be respected. As I campaigned, it wasn't uncommon to have conversations like the following with my campaign team:

> "Vikram. Good news! We received an invitation to the home of a party leader in Keene!"

> I'd reply to my team, exhausted from fundraising calls, "Keene? That's two hours away!"

> "Actually, it's probably longer, given it's tourist season and we'll probably hit traffic around the lakes."

"You're not helping!" I'd reply, exasperated. Then, more thoughtfully, I'd ask, "So, is this a house party? Are there going to be a lot of people there?"

"No, just her."

"Just her?"

"And maybe her husband."

"So, you want me to drive across the state to sit in the living room of just one person? Really?"

"And maybe her husband."

"Ah, right, and maybe her husband. So, you're asking me to drive across the state to talk to just these two people?"

"Yes, Vikram, that's what we're asking you to do. She's very influential. She knows a lot of people, and she's unlikely to drive out here."

My default is always a willingness to talk to anyone. And my team was telling me emphatically that it was worth my time to drive to Keene and talk with this one Granite Stater and maybe her husband.

"Okay, Let's go tomorrow."

There's a joke you don't hear much outside of New Hampshire about a local voter who is asked if they are going to vote for candidate X in the upcoming presidential election. "I don't know," the punch line has him reply, "I've only met him five times."

In New Hampshire, this is no joke!

So, I drove to this individual's house, and we met in her living room, where we had a lovely conversation, in the middle of which she told me that every presidential candidate in the last three cycles had sat in the same chair I was currently occupying. It's demanding for politicians to deal with voters who feel entitled to such individual attention, but it's also great. Far from making fun of the expectations of New Hampshire residents, the rest of America ought to feel equally entitled. In a representative democracy, people should be asking a lot of their politicians, and because of New Hampshire's unique importance in the electoral calendar, our moderate voter base, and our small size, we Granite Staters enjoy a relationship with political leaders that is much more directly democratic than that in many other states. I learned a lot about the day-to-day concerns of my fellow citizens—not just the rich donors but regular folks—and that is largely due to these face-to-face meetings.

What was actually troubling was how the retail politics of in-person interactions with the electorate failed to translate to the media. For a state so pivotal to American politics, New Hampshire had, at least during my campaign, one political reporter on local television, a few print journalists, and maybe two or three shows that addressed politics. The very qualities that make the state wonderfully conducive to little-*d* democratic politics—that is, its smaller population and think-for-yourself citizens—make it a tough media market for advertisers. We fall under the glare of national media with the political calendar, and to New Hampshire's modest local media is added a national media more concerned with ratings than actual reporting. Again and again, I encountered the reality that there was very little scrutiny of the claims made by politicians and virtually no fact-checking.

One consequence has been much discussed. Over the past four decades, America has seen more and more politicians who talk, behave, and perform for media moments. Less discussed is a consequence I became ever more attuned to. The media most liked those moments when politicians spoke with the conviction and passion of experts. The most attention went to the politician who offered, with conviction and unwavering commitment, the single solution to a complex problem. From national security to health care, from education to immigration, the certainty of a presumptive expert was rewarded the most minutes on television and radio, the most inches of column space. Embracing the inherent uncertainty as a means to expand the set of potential solutions to pressing challenges or discussing the nuances of policy constraints rarely got any attention.

Similar to what's happened to our national conversation, this has resulted in political debate tilting toward the extremes in both parties.

I witnessed many examples of this polarization during my campaign. For example, at one Republican town committee meeting, I spoke to a crowd of fifty people about some of the issues I was highlighting in my campaign: energy independence, fighting back against China, and containing runaway inflation. They asked relevant questions. I gave my best answers, showing, as best I could, how what I knew about China touched on what I understood about the economy, and vice versa. Out of the corner of my eye, I noticed my campaign staff smiling and nodding along. Then, about twenty-nine minutes into my allotted half hour, as I was answering what I thought was the last question, a woman in the back raised her hand.

"Vikram, your ideas obviously resonate with all of us. We love everything you're saying. However, it's all built on fraud. The election machines don't work. Our votes are being stolen. How can you think you'll have any impact, given all of this vote rigging that's taking place?"

With that question, I felt the room turn against me. I remember seeing multiple jaws drop on the faces of my campaign team. Thankfully, another speaker was scheduled immediately after me, so after sharing my belief that election integrity was a critical ingredient of democracy, my team quickly escorted me from the podium to my car.

Let me be clear. Not for a second do I dismiss people's sincere concerns, which is why I always engage everyone. Indeed, a burden of the generalist is not to ignore out of hand any opinion. At one level, the voter's suspicions made sense: if you deeply believe that an election was stolen and that future elections could still be rigged, then it is logical to be deeply angry about it, especially when so many people in trusted positions are telling you to distrust the government. What do you do with that anger, though? One person might choose to listen to a single expert and uncritically accept that expert's argument and evidence. Another person might turn to multiple experts, track down one or a few of the sources of their presented evidence, and begin to form her own opinion. The former lives in a world of experts on top. The latter keeps experts on tap. This is precisely why it's important for generalists to listen and engage people who disagree with them. The moment you refuse to see people as capable of being both-and or guest and host is the moment you reduce them to either-or, us and them. And that is the moment you cease being a generalist.

CHAPTER 37

Two Ears, One Mouth

Another stark example of polarization happened after the primaries, when I was no longer in the race. As the more consequential vote approached that would result in one candidate being chosen to represent the entire state for a six-year term, us-versus-them thinking and the left-versus-right chasm really opened. The spotlight was now centered on the general election candidates, but the same issues were still in play. However, the shades of gray around those issues had completely disappeared.

Nuance evaporated in the political debates and media reports. Rather than widening out to solutions, the conversation deteriorated into finger-pointing. It's easy to blame the press for this, and they certainly play a big role—but the problem is exacerbated by the politicians themselves, along with their handlers and experts. As the stakes became higher, outcomes began to trump process, and everything narrowed. It was a slippery slope.

This is the opposite of what a generalist works toward in any circumstance, but especially in an election. Even the American voter—so easily triggered and manipulated by either-or thinking in an us-versus-them environment—becomes complicit in this corrosion of a healthy political process. Polarization is a powerful weapon for those whose main goal is to win at all costs—even if the price is a slow erosion of the very democracy that makes elections possible in our country. It's one of the reasons why I decided to write this book to discuss the importance of the migrant mindset and the need to tap into the generalist approach we all can adopt. They enable us to discover and explore new ideas, viewpoints, and opinions.

Despite the challenges and some eye-opening moments that left me concerned about the state of our political process, I enjoyed many incredible experiences while I was running in the primaries. One of the real highlights during the middle of my campaign was that I secured the endorsements of some prominent Granite Staters. But the absolute most meaningful one of the bunch was received on Father's Day 2022 when, during a fiftieth-episode special, *The Kai Guy Show* broke with its policy of being nonpolitical and "entered politics" by endorsing me! Friends and colleagues were less enthused than I was, offering the counterfactual question: What if he hadn't endorsed me? Regardless, it meant a lot, and I remain super proud of the efforts Kai has made to maintain his podcast.

I remember one community that, more than any other, tested my generalist commitments. There is a group of Free Staters in New Hampshire, some of whom want to secede from the union. Yes, they want to leave the United States. They are so suspicious of and disenchanted with the American government, they are advocating separation. I was open to hearing their story, even as I was puzzled by their goal. You see, America, in my eyes, is the embodiment of a community that works well together. Every state contributes, and the whole is better off. The idea of secession seemed so far from practical or ideal, or so I felt, that I simply had to understand what made them think this might be a viable path.

During my campaign, there had been a little dustup between a delegation of Free Staters and the administration of a New Hampshire ski resort, Gunstock, owned by Belknap County. In the process, the resort was shut down, despite making money, employing locals, and serving many thousands of guests all year long. The conflict even drew in Governor Sununu and was dominating the local news. Seemingly randomly, one of the Free Staters who was part of the delegation reached out to me to see if I might help. "You're a business guy, and you seem willing to listen. We'd love your help to get the resort open again." I replied I would, of course, be willing to listen and viewed it as a good opportunity to learn more.

Advisers, friends, and family were aghast. Why in the world would I, running as a candidate for the US Senate, want to talk to people from a group that had members who didn't even want to be part of the United States? "Those people are crazy!" was the common refrain. Many years ago, such a statement would have been a snub, but such language in now regularly used to characterize those with whom we disagree.

I went ahead and met with a few members of the Belknap delegation and ultimately understood their perspective on the management of the Gunstock resort. While I ultimately chose not to engage with the issue, several members of the delegation told me how appreciative they were that I was willing to listen to them.

The moment we stop listening, even to secessionists, what options remain? One of the big lessons I took away from the whole process of running for office was that society would be a lot better if politicians did less talking and more listening. As my dad often reminded me when I was younger, "God gave you two ears and one mouth."

Since I didn't win the 2022 Republican primary, I never had the chance to challenge incumbent Maggie Hassen in the general election. Exit polls showed me with a high single-digit percentage of all votes, enough to be ahead of seven other candidates but coming in way behind General Don Bolduc, who won the primary with 36.8 percent. As one of the few political newbies, I think I was successful in connecting with people everywhere I went. But in the end, the polling experts said I was the second choice for voters who liked Bolduc as well as Chuck Morse, who finished second in the primary. This, I was told, was promising, even if disappointing, because it apparently demonstrated that my message was resonating. These experts said I'd entered the race too late, when many citizens had already committed to either Don or Chuck.

Despite not winning, I'll never regret my entry into politics. It was ultimately an invigorating and inspiring experience. But it was not without its disappointments, particularly in what it revealed about people and institutions I thought I knew well. At the time I ran, I had been teaching classes on economics, business, and decision-making at Yale and Harvard for thirteen years. The classes were popular, my reviews were consistently positive, and I had received numerous accolades for my teaching. Like many nontenured instructors, my contract was reevaluated on an annual basis. I'd never had a problem getting it renewed. In fact, prior to my Senate campaign, I had been in discussions with Harvard to deepen my engagement with the university as a professor of practice.

After I declared my candidacy as a Republican candidate for the US Senate, however, everything changed. I had assumed Harvard would support my interest in public service, as it had with other instructors at the university, such as Elizabeth Warren. But instead, my candidacy was met with passive derision, dismissal, and even some antagonism. Though I was aware of the long-established hostility toward conservative politics on liberal college campuses, what happened still shocked me. Not long after a senior colleague told me it was "disappointing" that I was running as a Republican, I received an email that my appointment would be over at the end of the term and my contract would not be renewed. The discussion of my becoming a professor of practice abruptly ended. In retrospect, I've come to think of this as a form of institutional cognitive dissonance: I was the son of immigrants, had degrees from prestigious schools, and was . . . drumroll, please . . . a Republican. The last part didn't fit the box I was supposed to be in.

These were all professional disappointments, and I dealt with them in stride. It was the personal gut punches that were emotionally painful. After I announced my candidacy, I was greeted with a flood of ugly diatribes from friends and former colleagues with whom I'd worked at Yale and Harvard, telling me they were "disgusted" by the fact that I was a Republican. The vitriol and venom stunned me. You would have thought I'd just joined the KKK, and perhaps to them, it seemed I had. Many of these colleagues—with whom I had worked, played squash, and enjoyed tailgates—literally could not believe that I was a lifelong Republican. Nothing about me had changed except the presumptive label others applied to me.

Indeed, as a generalist, I had been assiduous about keeping politics out of the classroom. And I've always worked hard to respect others' opinions. Listen, speak, then think for yourself, and invite others to do the same. Reciprocity, however, seems to be waning. For example, I'd been admonished by Harvard students and administrators for referring to America as a "melting pot" in one of my classes. For over a century, this metaphor was a normal way to celebrate America's shared cultural identity. And as the son of immigrants who say their proudest day was the day they became Americans, I happen to believe it's a useful image of the both-and qualities that make America great. Nevertheless, I was informed that I was being "insensitive" by using "identity-destroying" imagery. The better analogy, I was told, was America as a "mixed salad."

I was stunned and confused. I don't think the administrators were prepared for my next question.

"Why mixed salad over melting pot?" I asked, reminding them that the latter was first referenced in the late 1700s. Back then, it was European monarchies that deplored the idea that this new North American nation could unite humans from all over the world. Was the logic of "mixed salad," each element distinct and separate from the others, really a better description of America's promise?

No one at the university was interested in debating the point.

Not surprising to me, but noteworthy nonetheless, the nonprofit and nonpartisan Foundation for Individual Rights and Expression (FIRE) listed Harvard as the worst school in America for free speech in 2023. Sean Stevens, director of polling and analytics at FIRE, was quoted in the *New York Post* as saying, "We've done these rankings for years now, and Harvard is consistently near the bottom."

Unfortunately, there isn't a lot of time to stop and think on the campaign trail. It was month after month of eighteen-hour days. I had so much on my daily to-do lists that I took to not even driving my car. Someone else ferried me from event to event, and while they paid attention to traffic, I made calls, so very many calls. To media, to influencers, to funders, to advocates and critics. But even amid this busyness, again and again I applied my generalist approach to common pressing problems. And I published them, first as op-eds and eventually collected in a single volume, for all to see, consider, critique, and respond to.

Harvard wasn't the only one to dismiss me just because I had a political viewpoint—one that I'd spent a lifetime shaping through open exploration and continue to refine through continued exploration. Each time I published an opinion, I did so transparently to go on record and encourage a conversation. Instead of dialogue in response, I was called a climate-change denier, soft on immigration, even a "Taliban" when it came to women's rights. That I was none of those things didn't matter.

Even close friends surprised me. I reached out to a good friend whom I had known for more than twenty years. This was someone with whom I'd repeatedly and candidly explained my thoughts, beliefs, and opinions. After learning of my decision to run, he initially lauded my willingness to enter the public arena. Months later, he flatly declared he could not support my primary run.

"Why?" I asked.

"Because you're a Republican."

"And that matters, why?"

"Because you all think and vote the same."

Just a year earlier, I had literally published a book titled *Think for Yourself.* I had given him a copy. No matter. Someone I knew to be capable of being open-minded in every other aspect of his life couldn't do so when it came to politics.

CHAPTER 38

MULTIDIMENSIONAL THINKING

An unexpected consequence of my primary run was that a number of hopeful presidential candidates reached out to me. I like to think some of this was due to my having conducted myself as a candidate who was an active listener; wasn't afraid to offer my understanding of an issue or decision; and with the interests of New Hampshire and the country in mind, was willing to do my part. "Think freely, speak freely, listen freely, and afterward, act" could have been written above our front door. Presumably this was one reason why former US ambassador to the United Nations and South Carolina governor Nikki Haley was at our house mere days after she had declared her presidential candidacy. Along with all the obvious reasons to welcome Ambassador Haley to our home, there was also a personal one. Kai had just returned from a long weekend at Dartmouth College, where he had participated in a model United Nations. He was eager to chat with an actual participant at the real UN. To make that happen, we not only had Ambassador Haley over to speak about her presidential ambitions, but we also kept Kai home from school that day.

After Kristen and I welcomed our guests, the thirty or so people in the room had the opportunity to engage with Ambassador Haley in an off-the-record conversation about the leading policy issues of the day. As the youngest at the event, Kai was given the honor of asking the first question after her organized comments. He asked about global stability, how it had deteriorated, and what role America could or should play in making the world safe. Kristen and I beamed with pride. Ambassador Haley spent more than an hour with our little gathering and even took the time for a one-on-one conversation with Kai. It was a wonderful event—educational and inspirational—not just for Kai but for all of us in the room.

The next day, however, Kristen and I received an email from Kai's school. "We'll just need to know the specifics of Kai's absence to determine whether this is an excused or unexcused absence," wrote the school administrator. The school's question didn't sit well with us. We had alerted the school that Kai would be out for a "family event." Due to the politics of the day and the highly polarized nature of the world in which we lived—not to mention my recent campaign for the US Senate—broadcasting that a Republican presidential candidate was visiting our home might bother some at Kai's school or just come across as boastful. Instead, we kept our communication with the school simple: a family event. We were his parents, clearly had no interest in disrupting his education in any way, and in fact, consistently evidenced the opposite. Our goal was always to enhance our children's education. Why not assume we meant well? No matter what the administration believed, and perhaps it was just on bureaucratic autopilot, we now needed to defend our decision to pull Kai from school.

Coincidentally, I had invited Frank Edelblut, the commissioner of education for the state of New Hampshire, to the event. I had gotten to know Commissioner Edelblut and his wife a bit during my campaign and thought he would appreciate the invitation. I wasn't sure if he'd attend, but he not only attended and spoke with Governor Haley but also took some time to talk with Kai. Before he left, he half jokingly noted to Kristen and me that he was willing to write a letter to the school explaining Kai's absence if it would be helpful. When reading the email Kristen and I had received the next day, I took him up on his offer. Commissioner Edelblut obliged, penning a blissfully concise three-sentence letter that requested Kai be excused for his absence. Frank's eloquent middle sentence perfectly captured our feelings as parents: "Kai participated in an extracurricular civic activity vital to the future stability and vitality of our constitutional republic."

Even as I retype that sentence, I realize that every word of it is true. In many ways, it's an anchor statement about our democracy. We need to restore our collective responsibility for civic engagement to keep our republic vibrant and healthy. This sounds great, but it begs the question of how, especially amid the current political polarization in our country. It is a question I return to again and again.

How can a generalist improve what, to put it kindly, is suboptimal about American politics? A core value of the generalist's approach is acknowledgment and acceptance that individual perspectives on their own are limited, biased, and incomplete. As such, multiple perspectives are required to triangulate toward an understanding of any issue. This implies multidimensional thinking, not just about ideas and problems but also about the way we view each other. As unique, individual combinations of experiences, beliefs, and circumstances, we each have something to contribute. It doesn't make sense to segment that individuality into either this bucket or that one. Sure, a person might be conservative or liberal, but that's just one dimension of their personality and belief system. Our civic health would be greatly improved by more multidimensional thinking about our fellow Americans and the challenges we must all confront together.

A lot of what prevents politics from working better, my generalist brain believes, can be attributed to the way we have all been conditioned to approach politics as a single dimension. We are told there is a "left" and a "right" and a line connecting these two points. Along that line is a "spectrum" of different political attitudes—a middle, two extremes, and positions in between—that can be used to position each of us. Each of us is conservative or liberal. It's very either-or thinking: either you are to my right or to my left. This is what I've fought against my whole life—the labels, the boxes, the narrow thinking. It's a flat and unsatisfying approach, and it's not the type of thinking I routinely encounter among my fellow Granite Staters. In fact, I rarely see this type of one-dimensional thinking in America, except when it comes to politics. On this important topic, unfortunately, one-dimensional thinking is ubiquitous and, I believe, destructive to healthy civic engagement.

We need more dimensions, not fewer. Instead of just left and right, red and blue, we need open-minded listeners and collaborative problem solvers from all political persuasions. We need people who seek more and richer information so that they can think and act on the *best* available evidence. When new data emerge, these people reassess. Above all else, open-minded people remain skeptical of their own assumptions and are willing to change their minds if they are convinced to do so. Given the inherent willingness they have to accept the potential of being wrong, the open-minded tend to listen closely to those with whom they disagree, regardless of whether they are described as left or right, Democrat or Republican.

Closed-minded thinkers, on the other hand, are dogmatic. Regardless of the information presented, they are unwilling to reassess. Even in the face of contradictory evidence, they characterize new information as "good" or "bad," depending on its role in bolstering or undermining their views. They "explore" ideas in a silo of like-minded thinkers with whom they already agree. This may lead to affirmation, but it rarely, if ever, leads to a better understanding of an issue. In an ever-changing world, how can you find new solutions to complex problems if you're never open to challenging your current understanding of an issue?

Another dimension we might consider is an individual's commitment to process over outcomes. As a generalist, I see the same patterns in our national discourse that I saw in business and academia earlier in my career. People who focused solely on outcomes rarely added value, whereas those protective of the process of data-driven decision-making were often able to solve tough problems. Think back to the earlier description of selecting students for my business ethics class. We had battles over how students would be selected, but once we settled on a transparent process, everyone accepted the outcome—even if disappointed that some didn't make the cut. It was the *process* that guaranteed legitimacy and acceptance of outcomes.

While most Americans live most of their lives in multiple dimensions, more and more of our politics is restricted to only one. It isn't accidental. I know my own instance best, so I will speak to it. One organization that exercised enormous financial influence in the 2022 New Hampshire Republican primary race was the Democratic Party. That's right, a major player in the GOP primary was the Democratic Party. The election was scheduled for September, and in August, polling showed an open race with equal opportunities for all contenders to get their messages out to potential voters. Shortly thereafter, the Democrats outspent every candidate in the Republican primary on advertising and marketing to promote candidates they wanted to run against. Their "pick our opponent" strategy worked, and Democrats won the Senate seat and both congressional seats.

Do American voters win when this is how the game is played? Decidedly not. But it's a clear indication of just how easy it has become to manipulate voters. I fully recognize that this type of political gamesmanship is played by both parties—and it's very worrisome. But as I've mentioned, even American voters are complicit in this political charade. Our one-dimensional approach has made it very easy to herd us in one direction or the other, to compel us to make either-or decisions. It makes people feel like they're taking a stand, but in reality, they're just being herded along, albeit with a lot of attitude.

Our polarization is being weaponized and used against us. It takes almost nothing to trigger us and send us running for our boxes—labels flying and fingers pointing. This makes it easy for the closed-minded, outcome-focused thinkers to manipulate us and achieve their objectives, regardless of whether or not they are helping our country. And while that's highly concerning, think about the leverage our polarization gives to those who wish to weaken our democracy or gain power over America. The implications are profound, and if not addressed, they could be destabilizing to the future of the United States.

America needs more multidimensional, open-minded thinkers with a stronger commitment to the principles of process over predetermined outcomes. Instead of right and left, perhaps we can think of people as open-minded or not, as process or outcome oriented. Simply adding those dimensions is surely a step forward in the right direction of moving beyond our dangerously polarized state.

Let's shake the labels and table the tactics. Our democracy requires us all to step out of our silos and open our minds. That's how we tackle complex problems *together*. There is immense strength in our collective wisdom and unsettling weakness in our divisiveness. My love for New Hampshire and America is due to my fellow citizens demonstrating what must be done. Think freely, speak freely, listen freely, and do your part. This is the foundation not only of being a generalist but also of being a good citizen in a democratic nation.

Conclusion

The Journey Is the Answer

My wife, Kristen, and I have been married since 2001. Even after all this time together, we still don't agree on everything—and that's an understatement! We consider ourselves open-minded problem-solvers, but we both have strong opinions on most topics. What should we have for dinner? Where do you want to spend the holidays this year? Do you think it's time to replace the roof? What do you think is the best way to save for our children's education? Once in a while, we offer the same answer, but most of the time, we see things differently. We converse, debate, and sometimes disagree. It's just who we are. We listen to each other and work through our divergent views until ultimately arriving at a consensus. If one of us slips into either-or thinking or starts labeling the other's ideas, we stop and reset.

We're still a work in progress, but it's a discipline we've adopted over the years. I know we're not alone in our never-ending pursuit of marital harmony. In households across the country, millions of couples are answering similar questions while relaxing in their living rooms, eating dinner together, or sitting on their front porches after work. For some, such questions cause rising tensions or even heated arguments. For others—even those who disagree—open dialogue, respect, and empathetic listening lead to thoughtful consideration and collaboration in order to arrive at the best answers.

Decision-making inputs and outcomes are as unique as the individuals involved in the conversation. What's the same is that we're all navigating uncertainty when we try to answer these questions. As simple and imperfect as it may be, a process of some sort is required to sift through all the options, and *how* we get to an answer is as important as the answer itself. It doesn't take a genius to see which approach leads to better answers—and happier marriages. Clearly, "It's my way or the highway" does not foster consensus or strengthen relationships. Over time, self-centered, one-dimensional thinking rips couples apart—it's sad but true. And though we may recognize that more both-and thinking and collaborative problem-solving is the best approach, it's not always easy to execute in the heat of the moment. As a generalist with a capital *G* who is always swimming against the current, I know this all too well.

But what about when the scope is wider? What happens when the problem is broader and the parties trying to answer the question don't know each other well? This, too, is happening across our country. How can San Francisco, California, deal with homelessness? What's the best way for El Paso, Texas, to handle illegal immigration? What are some steps that Memphis, Tennessee, can take to prevent violent crime? How might Columbus, Ohio, combat air pollution? Or how can tiny Grafton, New Hampshire, deal with its bear problem? If you're an either-or thinker, you start your answer with the politicians or political parties who run these cities. But if you're a generalist, you look at the history of the problem, examine the contributing factors, and talk to a wide variety of stakeholders. You recognize the complexities and gather diverse perspectives and opinions. Most of all, you remain authentically curious and mind your own biases.

When looking at a problem as a generalist, it's as much about the process of discovery as the answer. Think deeply about this statement. I've mentioned this multiple times for a reason. I'm saying

The Making of a Generalist

emphatically that the process *is* the answer—no matter the question. Genuine problem-solving, whatever the topic, requires multidimensional thinking across several areas of expertise. If you're looking at issues through a narrow political prism guided by either-or thinking, each problem immediately becomes left or right—Republican or Democrat. This means every insight, fact, or perspective you encounter around the issue gets labeled, dropped in a particular box, and either accepted or dismissed based on the source of the information.

You already have your answer, despite the fact that you might know it's biased and incomplete. It doesn't matter which side of the aisle informs your opinion. That's not the point. The point is that your journey from point A to point B was cut short—and that's a damn shame, because a longer journey would have led you to a more informed answer, a better answer. "A foolish consistency is the hobgoblin of little minds," Ralph Waldo Emerson's famous line, seems an apt description of what's happening today. We've come to prize consistency over truth, and when we dismiss ideas inconsistent with our views, we close the door to fresh solutions to some of our very real problems.

In keeping with some of the major challenges we currently face, let's raise the stakes even higher. Let's take our questions to the national level, where the dynamics get even more interesting, complex, and important to understand. First, for sure, almost no one knows each other at this level. And human nature tells us not to trust strangers, even those with shared American values. This trust gap makes it easy to slap labels on each other, instantly polarizing the situation. Sound familiar? Second, the questions and answers have a much bigger impact. At this level, we're discussing things like national security, the economy, and even global stability. Americans have immense influence in the world, so when we take on big issues, people across the planet start holding their breath.

Who should be our next president? How is global warming affecting the planet? Do we have a clear response outlined for the next pandemic? What's the best way to handle inflation and the national debt? What are our best options for responding to wars in Ukraine, Israel, or elsewhere? How would you describe our current approach to answering such questions as a nation? Are we capable of collaboration, or are we a nation at war with itself? Do we listen with authentic curiosity and respect to America's many diverse stakeholders, or do we put people in boxes and dismiss their ideas? Do we narrow our information gathering to our political, cultural, professional, and socioeconomic silos, or do we open our minds and listen and learn from the cacophony of perspectives that make up our wonderful country? Do we follow the herd instead of listening hard and being heard? Remember, the answers to these (and other) questions will affect the lives of more than 330 million citizens. Yet, according to Pew Research, 65 percent of Americans say they always or often feel exhausted when *thinking* about politics—before they even enter the conversation. Believe me, I can relate—and I've run for political office!

Is anyone really surprised by this statistic, given the binary, us-versus-them mentality that dominates today's political discourse? I get the reluctance—even anxiety and sense of exhaustion—but it can't be an excuse for nonparticipation. In today's unsteady world, there are too many important questions awaiting well-considered answers. Embrace the friction—it is one of the most important gifts of democracy—and jump in with an open mind. Besides, no matter what anyone says, we have way more things in common than things that divide us. Think freely, listen openly, and contribute constructively. Then, take this new mindset back to your community, back to your home, and back to your partner—because it's much bigger than politics. It's a way of being.

As Judge William Hastie eloquently noted, "Democracy is a process, not a static condition. It is becoming, rather than being. It can easily be lost, but never is fully won. Its essence is eternal struggle." No truer words have been spoken. We would all do well to take this advice. Forget about the destination and just keep improving the journey. We can't let our squabbles diminish our liberties. We must honor our responsibilities as keepers of the flame, stewards of a country that still attracts people from every corner of the world, just as it did my parents. Part of that responsibility is open-mindedness and listening with the intent to fully understand. This is the common courtesy I was taught as a young child of immigrant parents who were guests in a new land.

Though I didn't realize it when I was young, the lessons my parents taught me were invaluable. Either intentionally or unintentionally, they guided me toward my life's path as a generalist—and this is where I found my calling. At some point along that path, I learned that being a generalist is not a destination; it's an ongoing journey, a mindset, a way of living.

No matter who you are, where you come from, or how the world tries to label you, your journey is unique and holds infinite wisdom for those willing to listen and try to understand. Offer others this same courtesy, and you'll have the opportunity to learn from their infinite wisdom as well. That's why, for me, being a generalist means listening deeply to many ideas, perspectives, and opinions before forming my own. And once I've formed an opinion, I immediately remind myself of my own biases, my limitations, and the incompleteness of my individual understanding of an issue. Like everyone, I'm a work in progress. But every day of my life, I strive to practice this important discipline. Remaining curious, humble, and open-minded is key.

Like the fox that benefits from gathering as much information from as many sources as possible, Americans must once again open their minds and hearts to one another. In my opinion, the future of our nation depends on it. There's a reason why Gouverneur Morris, a Pennsylvania delegate to the 1787 Constitutional Convention in Philadelphia and one of America's Founding Fathers, penned the phrase "to form a more perfect union" in the preamble to the US Constitution. He was explicitly describing a process of constant improvement, a never-ending journey toward an elusive perfect. This is why I remind myself daily that I am one human seeking to learn from many. None of us is flawless, but we are stronger when we listen openly to each other and work together toward a more perfect union. *This* is the way of the generalist, the way of the fox, and the way I have learned to successfully navigate our uncertain world.

Acknowledgments

In today's increasingly complex world, it's extremely rare to accomplish anything on your own. This book is no exception. The number of people who have contributed to my life and the lessons learned along the way are too numerous to mention. Nevertheless, some individuals deserve special acknowledgment for having had a disproportionate influence on this project.

I've been blessed to have supportive friends and family, caring mentors, insightful students, engaging clients, dedicated employees, welcoming neighbors, and encouraging colleagues who have helped me at every stage of my journey. Because many of the most important people in my life are mentioned in the book, I will refrain from listing all of them here.

With that said, I cannot thank my family enough for their support and for tolerating my frequent disappearances to write. I want to especially thank my ever-patient wife Kristen, my always encouraging daughter Tori, and my constantly curious son Kai. I can't imagine three better companions on life's journey. I also owe a great debt of gratitude to my parents Vishnu and Shobha, who sacrificed at every stage of life to ensure that I had opportunities, and my sister Vanita, who has always been supportive.

My campaign for the United States Senate introduced me to many good people across the political spectrum, most of whom were encouraging and supportive of my effort to get elected. I also met some folks who were less encouraging, more dismissive, and far more dogmatic than expected. I want to thank them, too, for they helped me fully appreciate the need for constructive, civil, and open-minded dialogue—especially when opinions differ. All of us could learn to listen more and talk less.

Lastly, many people helped pull this book together. I want to explicitly thank Rob Varsalone for his invaluable counsel and comments on early drafts of the manuscript. And I remain grateful for the assistance of Thomas LeBien, Amanda Moon, and Jeff Alexander at Moon & Company as well as Kathy Meis and Shilah LaCoe at Bublish. Their editorial and production assistance made it possible for me to remain in control of the book while securing expert input from some of the most capable professionals in publishing.

Manufactured by Amazon.ca
Acheson, AB